T0291556

Death and Funeral Practices in Poland

This book provides a shortform definitive reference text on funerary practice in Poland. An overview of the important features of the Polish funeral law, funerals, cremations, cemeteries, and funeral industry, the book also covers the demographic characteristic of mortality in Poland.

Drawing on original empirical research, the book is interdisciplinary, which facilitates further transnational comparative research on this important topic. It is the first book to offer a broad look at the evolution and current status of Polish funerary practices. It provides an essential summary to researchers with an interest in funeral practices in Poland. Some of the areas explored are the country's historical development, the contemporary legal framework and how Poland manages its cemeteries, crematoria and other death spaces. Built on original ethnographic research conducted by the authors, this book interprets the predominance of Catholic funerals, examines the relatively recent history of cremation, and contextualizes the practices of commemoration and memoralisation.

This interdisciplinary book will be of interest to academics, policymakers and practitioners interested in the historic, geographic, demographic, (multi)cultural and political context in which the funerary practices in Poland have developed, as well as the technical and professional aspects of the industry.

Anna E. Kubiak is a Professor at the Institute of Philosophy and Sociology, Polish Academy of Sciences, Poland, and a Lecturer at the Graduate School for Social Research, Warsaw, Poland.

Anna Długozima is an Assistant Professor at the Institute of Environmental Engineering at WULS, Warsaw, Poland.

Agnieszka Wedel-Domaradzka works at the Faculty of Law and Economics at Kazimierz Wielki University, Poland.

Routledge International Focus on Death and Funeral Practices
Series Editor: Julie Rugg
University of York, UK

Death Studies is an international and interdisciplinary endeavour and encompasses an interest in all mortality-related themes. This series of shortform books provides essential information on death and funeral practices in countries throughout the world.

Fully referenced, and supported by relevant images, figures and tables, books in the series provide an essential research resource on practices, the law, and funeral-related procedures around the world. Collectively, the series provides an invaluable framework for international comparison.

This series is a continuation of *Funerary International*, a series distributed by Emerald Publishing. Four books were published in this legacy series: *Funerary Practices in England and Wales* (Rugg & Parsons, 2018); *Funerary Practices in the Netherlands* (Mathijssen & Venhorst, 2019); *Funerary Practices in the Czech Republic* (Nešporová, 2021); and *Funerary Practices in Serbia* (Pavićević, 2021).

Death and Funeral Practices in Russia
Sergei Mokhov

Death and Funeral Practices in Portugal
Rafaela Ferraz Ferreira, Ana Júlia Almeida Miranda and Francisco Queiroz

Death and Funeral Practices in Poland
Edited by Anna E. Kubiak, Anna Długozima and Agnieszka Wedel-Domaradzka

For more information on the series please visit: www.routledge.com/ Routledge-International-Focus-on-Death-and-Funeral-Practices/book-series/DEATH

Death and Funeral Practices in Poland

Edited by Anna E. Kubiak,
Anna Długozima and
Agnieszka Wedeł-Domaradzka

Routledge
Taylor & Francis Group

LONDON AND NEW YORK

First published 2024
by Routledge
4 Park Square, Milton Park, Abingdon, Oxon OX14 4RN

and by Routledge
605 Third Avenue, New York, NY 10158

Routledge is an imprint of the Taylor & Francis Group, an informa business

© 2024 selection and editorial matter, Anna E. Kubiak, Anna Długozima and Agnieszka Wedeł-Domaradzka; individual chapters, the contributors

The right of Anna E. Kubiak, Anna Długozima and Agnieszka Wedeł-Domaradzka to be identified as the authors of the editorial material, and of the authors for their individual chapters, has been asserted in accordance with sections 77 and 78 of the Copyright, Designs and Patents Act 1988.

All rights reserved. No part of this book may be reprinted or reproduced or utilised in any form or by any electronic, mechanical, or other means, now known or hereafter invented, including photocopying and recording, or in any information storage or retrieval system, without permission in writing from the publishers.

Trademark notice: Product or corporate names may be trademarks or registered trademarks, and are used only for identification and explanation without intent to infringe.

British Library Cataloguing-in-Publication Data
A catalogue record for this book is available from the British Library

ISBN: 978-1-032-07552-5 (hbk)
ISBN: 978-1-032-07553-2 (pbk)
ISBN: 978-1-003-20763-4 (ebk)

DOI: 10.4324/9781003207634

Typeset in Times New Roman
by MPS Limited, Dehradun

Contents

Figures

Tables

Abbreviations

CBOS	Centrum Badania Opinii Społecznej [Public Opinion Research Center]
ECtHR	The European Court of Human Rights
FIAT-IFTA	Fédération Internationale des Associations de Thanatologues (FIAT) – International Federation of Thanatologists Associations (IFTA)
GUS	Główny Urząd Statystyczny [Statistics Poland]
mpzp	miejscowy plan zagospodarowania przestrzennego [local spatial development plan]
NGO	organizacja pozarządowa [non-governmental organization]
NID	Narodowy Instytut Dziedzictwa [National Heritage Board of Poland]
NIK	Naczelna Izba Kontroli [Supreme Audit Office]
NSA	Naczelny Sąd Administracyjny [Supreme Administrative Court]
PESEL	Powszechny Elektroniczny System Ewidencji Ludności [Universal Electronic Civil Registration System]
PLN	Polish zloty
PIP	Polska Izba Pogrzebowa [Polish Funeral Chamber]
PSP	Polskie Stowarzyszenie Pogrzebowe [Polish Funeral Association]
SARP	Stowarzyszenie Architektów Polski [the Association of Polish Architects]
SN	Sąd Najwyższy [Supreme Court]
suikzpg	studium uwarunkowań i kierunków zagospodarowania przestrzennego gminy [study of conditions and directions for spatial development]
UCChZ	Ustawa o cmentarzach i chowaniu zmarłych [Cemeteries and Burials of the Deceased Act]
WWI	First World War

WWII	Second World War
ZSRR	Związek Socjalistycznych Republik Radzieckich, Związek Radziecki [USRR – Union of Soviet Socialist Republics]
ZUS	Zakład Ubezpieczeń Społecznych [Social Insurance Institution in Poland]

Contributors

Anna Długozima is a landscape architect, planner, graduate of Spatial Development at the Warsaw University of Life Sciences (WULS-SGGW) and the Faculty of Journalism and Political Science, Institute of International Relations at the University of Warsaw, and an Assistant Professor at WULS, Warsaw, Poland. She is the author of the book *Cmentarze jako ogrody żywych i umarłych* (Cemeteries as Gardens of the Living and the Dead). Her research interests include protection and designing of cemeteries. In 2017–2021, she was a member of the Central Conservation Commission attached to the General Monument Conservator in the Ministry of Culture and National Heritage. In 2016–2021 she was the principal investigator of the National Science Centre Poland grant Planning cemeteries in the existing urban and rural structures in Poland, seen from the spatial order aspect, against the background of the contemporary sepulchral space.

Anna E. Kubiak is a sociologist and a cultural anthropologist, a Professor at the Institute of Philosophy and Sociology, Polish Academy of Sciences, Poland, and a lecturer at the Graduate School for Social Research, Warsaw, Poland. She is the author of books including *INNE ŚMIERCI. Antropologia Umierania i Żałoby w Późnej Nowoczesności* (OTHER DEATHS. Anthropology of Dying and Mourning in Late Modernity) (Warszawa 2014), *Pogrzeby to Nasze Życie* (Funerals Are Our Lives) (Warszawa 2015), and *Assisted Death in the Age of Biopolitics and Bioeconomy* (Cambridge Scholars Publishing 2020). Her research interests include death studies, biopolitics, bioeconomy, social trauma, the Fourth Age of global ageing societies, visual anthropology, and animal studies. For more author information, see https://ifispan.pl/members/akubiakifispan-waw-pl/.

Piotr Szukalski is an associate professor at the University of Lodz, Lodz, Poland. His research interests are population ageing, family caregiving, older adults activities, ageism, intergenerational relations, and regional demography. He has published more than 250 articles and chapters related to social gerontology, demography, intergenerational relations and family issues. He is a member of the Committee on Demographic Studies, Polish Academy of Sciences, and Committee on Forecasting, Polish Academy of Sciences, the National Council for Development at the President of the Republic of Poland, The Governmental Council for Population Policy at the Polish Prime Minister (vice-chairman), and the Council for Senior Policy at the Polish Minister of Family and Social Policy (Vice-chairman).

Agnieszka Wedel-Domaradzka received a PhD in international law from Nicolaus Copernicus University, and is employed at Kazimierz Wielki University in the Faculty of Law and Economics in Poland. Her research focuses on human rights in the context of the right to life, private and family life, and vulnerable groups' rights. She is the author of more than 80 human rights and international law publications and is the author of the monograph *Death and Human Rights*. She has also completed a grant from the National Science Centre dedicated to the 'Legal aspects of burial – international and national standards in the face of contemporary challenges'. She is currently working on the topic of the concept of the best interests of the child in ECHR jurisprudence.

Acknowledgments

We appreciate the support of many academics and other persons in writing this book.

We are deeply thankful to Julie Rugg, who invited us to the Funerary International Series and who put in a great deal of work to help us prepare the proposal. What is more, from the very start she offered advice in all substantive matters. We are also especially grateful to Krzysztof Wolicki, president of the Polish Funeral Association, who shared his materials about the funerary industry and always answered all questions concerning these issues. We express our deep appreciation to Elżbieta Morawska, the chief editor of the publishing house of the Institute of Philosophy and Sociology, Polish Academy of Sciences, who granted permission to use excerpts from the book *Pogrzeby to Nasze Życie* (Funerals are Our Lives) by Anna E. Kubiak, released by this publisher in 2015. We are pleased to present up-to-date data on burial law, planning and designing cemeteries, and the funeral industry, which was possible thanks to the implementation of grants funded by the National Science Center, Poland: 'Planning cemeteries in the existing urban and rural structures in Poland, seen from the spatial order aspect, against the background of the contemporary sepulchral space' (principal investigator Anna Długozima), 'Legal aspects of burial – international and national standards in the face of contemporary challenges' (principal investigator Agnieszka Wedeł-Domaradzka), and 'The evolution of the funeral culture in Poland. The funeral industry perspective' (principal investigator Anna E. Kubiak).

1 Poland

Introduction

Anna Długozima, Anna E. Kubiak, and Agnieszka Wedel-Domaradzka

Poland, officially the Republic of Poland (RP), along with Bulgaria, Croatia, the Czech Republic, Estonia, Hungary, Latvia, Lithuania, Romania, Slovakia, and Slovenia is counted among the cultural and civilization realm of Central Europe (Smętkowski, Wójcik 2009; Winnicki 2017). Poland's area is 312,696 square kilometers, which ranks 9th in size in Europe. In 2021, Poland's population was 38,179,800 (GUS 2021), placing it 8th in Europe (Figure 1.1).

Poland is characterized by a diverse landscape. Protected areas make up 20% of the country's area (GUS 2019). Poland is located between the Baltic Sea in the north and the Sudeten and Carpathian Mountains in the south.

Poland is characterized by a polycentric spatial structure. In addition to Warsaw – the capital with a population of 1.8 million – the largest urban centers include Katowice, Kraków, Łódź, Poznań, and Wrocław – each inhabited by more than 500,000 people. The raw material industrial regions of southwestern Poland, i.e., Silesia (hard coal, zinc, and lead ores) and Legnica (copper basin), also tend to create spatial clusters. They are among the most industrialized areas in Central Europe. Poland is also one of the leading agricultural producers in the EU.

Poland experienced partitioning (1772–1918), during which its lands were divided up among three neighboring empires. The northern, western, and southwestern areas of the country were partitioned by Prussia, the southern and southeastern areas were annexed by Austria, and the central and eastern Polish territories became part of Russia. To this day, the diversity of infrastructure and spatial layout, but also the status and development of cemeteries that arose during the partition period, is discernible (Rogowska 2014; NIK 2016 Długozima 2020; Staszyńska 2020).

Before WWII, the Polish lands were famous for the diversity of their ethnic communities. WWII, which began with Germany's attack on Poland on September 1, 1939, brought severe destruction to that mosaic,

DOI: 10.4324/9781003207634-1

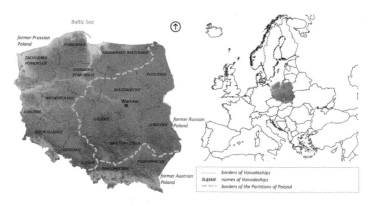

Figure 1.1 The location of Poland in the context of Europe, taking into account the administrative division and the partitions of Poland. Prepared by the authors using QGIS3 tools.

as Poland's Jewish population was almost completely annihilated in the Holocaust. Overall, more than 6 million Polish citizens were killed. However, cemeteries still bear witness to the multiculturalism of prewar times. On Polish soil today are cemeteries of the following nationalities and ethnic groups: Jewish, Ukrainian (including Lemko and Boyko), Tatar, wartime cemeteries – Russian, German, British, and Italian – as well as single graves of Roma and Armenians. In addition to Roman Catholic cemeteries, there are cemeteries of other faiths: Jewish, Protestant, Greek Catholic, Orthodox, Old Believers, Old Catholic Mariavite Church, Tatar, and Karaite. Many of these cemeteries are deteriorating, and only recently have activists from various associations, along with volunteers, taken up the task of restoring them.

In the late 1990s, Poland was held up as a success story in the democratic transition underway behind the former Iron Curtain a process that resulted in its admission to the European Union in 2004. On the basis of the Constitution of the Republic of Poland adopted in 1997, it is an example of a parliamentary republic based on the tripartite division of legislative, executive, and judicial power. Local government in Poland is organized at three levels: provincial (16), district (314), and municipal (2,477) (GUS 2021). The basic territorial unit and the basic link of the spatial planning system is the municipality, which carries out public tasks of local importance, related to meeting the collective needs of the local community (Niewiadomski 2003). Authorities at the municipal level are responsible for such tasks as technical infrastructure, social infrastructure, order, and environmental protection, including green areas and cemeteries.

References

Długozima Anna 2020, "Social Infrastructure of Burial Nature in Poland by Voivodeships – Conditions and Changes", *Acta Sci. Pol. Administratio Locorum*, 19(1), 21–34

GUS Główny Urząd Statystyczny (Statistics Poland) 2021. https://stat.gov.pl/en/basic-data/ [21.10.2021]

GUS 2019, "Poland in the European Union. A statistical portrait, Statistical Products Department". http://stat.gov.pl [21.10.2021]

Niewiadomski Zbigniew 2003, *Planowanie przestrzenne. Zarys systemu* (Spatial Planning. System outline), Wydawnictwo LexisNexis, Warszawa

NIK 2016, Zarządzanie cmentarzami komunalnymi (Management of municipal cemeteries). https://www.nik.gov.pl/plik/id,12230,vp,14613.pdf [10.04.2022]

"Poland in the European Union. A statistical portrait, Statistical Products Department" 2019. http://stat.gov.pl [21.10.2021]

Rogowska Barbara 2014, "Stanowisko władz komunistycznych w latach siedemdziesiątych XX wieku w zakresie cmentarnictwa wyznaniowego i komunalnego" (The position of the communist regime on the religious and communal cemeteries in the 1970s.), Annales Universitatis Paedagogicae Cracoviensis. Studia Politologica XIII, 165, 75–93

Smętkowski Maciej, Wójcik Piotr 2009, "Regiony w Europie Środkowo-Wschodniej: Tendencje i Czynniki Rozwojowe" (Regional Development in Central and Eastern European Countries: Trends and Factors), *Raporty i analizy EUROREG*, 3, Centrum Europejskich Studiów Regionalnych i Lokalnych EUROREG, Warszawa. https://www.euroreg.uw.edu.pl/dane/web_euroreg_publications_files/2725/smtkowski,_wjcik_(2009)_regiony_w_ew_-_tendencje_i_czynniki_rozwojowe.pdf [21.10.2021]

Staszyńska Maria 2020, "Regionalne zróżnicowanie pochówków w Polsce" (The Regional Diversification of Burials in Poland), *Przegląd Socjologii Jakościowej*, 16(4), 210–231

Winnicki Zdzisław 2017, "Europa Środkowa czy Europa Środkowo-Wschodnia? Europejskie kręgi cywilizacyjne" (Eastern or Central-Eastern Europe? European civilization circles), *Wschodnioznawstwo*, 11, 11–20

2 History

Anna E. Kubiak,
Agnieszka Wedeł-Domaradzka, and
Anna Długozima

Funerary Culture in Poland: Slavic and Christian Traditions

As Juliusz Chróścicki (1974, 84) notes, the formula of the modern funeral rite in Poland was influenced by Slavic burial culture traditions, as well as Christian ones dating back to the Middle Ages. The author reconstructs the main elements of a Slavic funeral. After the death of a relative, the whole family kept vigil by the deceased. Then he was escorted to a 'żalnik', which is a pagan cemetery.[1] The funeral procession included hired weepers, who lamented, tore their robes, and hurt themselves until they bled. People who died a violent, sudden death were buried at crossroads or in the woods. In the northwestern regions of the country, the bodies of the dead were burned. This ritual was connected with Lusatian culture, and, among the Slavs, it was connected with the cult of the sun and fire. Along with the deceased, everyday objects such as pottery, ornaments, tools, and clothing were burned. The burnt human bones, after washing, were deposited into vessels called ashtrays, which were designed for this purpose, (Łuka 1956, 27) (Figure 2.1).

During the Middle Ages, the Church fought against this custom, as well as against burials at crossroads and in forests. However, as with other ceremonies of family and annual rituals, the Church adopted some customs. Archaic forms were preserved in folk customs described by Fisher (1921) and Biegeleisen (1930), among others.

The most intensive ritualization of funerals in Europe took place in the 17th century. In Poland at that time, pompa funebris, also known as *apparatus funebris* (Chróścicki 1974, 8), known throughout Europe, took place. These were funerals of kings, magnates, and noblemen. The following phases can be distinguished in the evolution of burials in postwar Poland (Kubiak 2015).

1 The communist period's modest funerals, organized in cities by municipal funeral homes, and in the countryside with the traditional help of neighbors.

DOI: 10.4324/9781003207634-2

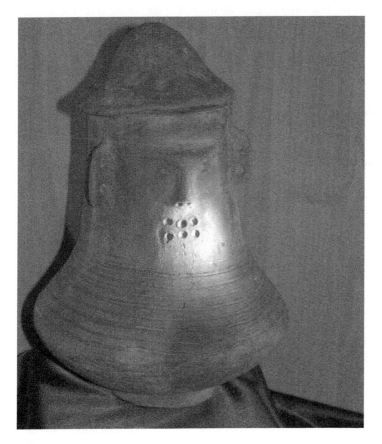

Figure 2.1 Ashtray in the museum in Międzyrzecz. Photograph by Anna E. Kubiak.

2 In the 1990s, with the emergence of private funeral companies, the burial becomes more opulent, with rich decorum, musical setting, changes in the appearance of the coffin, and the assistance of elegant funeral workers.
3 In the 21st century, some traditional elements of the rural funeral disappear, and this is associated with the funeral parlor taking control over the body. For example, the practice of keeping the body at home and having relatives watch over the deceased for three days is disappearing. After the year 2000, multimedia (films and photos about the deceased) and digital memorials are added.

4   Many Poles who watched the funerals of the victims of the catastrophe in Smolensk in 2010 were inspired to want more ceremonial rituals and expensive hearses.
5   On the first of March 2011, the funeral allowance was reduced. This affects the abandonment of some elements of the funeral, which now becomes somewhat more modest.

Chronology of Major Legislation

Legal regulations concerning cemeteries and the burial of the dead were enacted relatively soon after Poland regained its independence in 1918. In 1919, legal action was issued on the subject of cemeteries. This was the Basic Sanitary Act of July 19, 1919. According to this Act, the entities that were obliged to establish and maintain communal mortuaries and cemeteries and to take care of them, as well as to arrange for the maintenance of burial grounds, were the so-called local government bodies (Art 3, Act of 19 July 1919). Administratively, these activities were under the Ministry of Public Health (Art. 2, Act of 19 July 1919), which regulate the transportation and exhumation of corpses also (Ordinance of the Ministry of Public Health of 6 May 1920).

Dedicated to the issue of burying the dead, the law was enacted in 1932 (Act of 17 March 1932; Dziobek-Romański 1998). This regulation included provisions on the declaration of death, burials, cemeteries, and the exhumation of corpses. The declaration of death had to be reflected in the death certificate, which was also a necessary document for burial. A catalog of persons entitled to burial included the members of the deceased's immediate family in the following order: surviving spouse or spouses of descendants, relatives in the ascending line, collateral relatives to the fourth degree of kinship, and relatives in the direct line to the first degree. The right to burial by the competent military authorities was also granted to military persons who died in active military service or in a state of retirement, and to participants in national uprisings.

The law also regulates the possible modes of burial by defining them as burial by interment in earth pits, masonry graves or church or cemetery catacombs, and sinking into the sea.

According to the regulations adopted, cemeteries had to be in a fenced area suitable for sanitary purposes. This right authority also had the power to close cemeteries. In the case of a Catholic church, the consent of the clerical authority was necessary (Art. XIV, Concordat between the Holy See and the Republic of Poland, 1925).

A funeral home or mortuary was obligatory in cemeteries. The establishment, expansion, and closure of secular cemeteries was the responsibility of a municipality or an association of municipalities established for this purpose. The use of cemeteries and cemetery facilities was subject to payment to religious associations, legal persons, and the municipality running the cemetery.

In the case of burial in a denominational cemetery, the manager of that cemetery decided, with the proviso, that burial could not be refused to a person who was not of a particular religion if there was no municipal cemetery within 30 kilometers of where the burial could take place. A time limit was set to allow the reuse of a burial ground after 20 years from the last burial date. This period could be extended upon payment of a fee. The burial ground was available for reuse 50 years after the last burial and subject to the transfer of remains and the preservation of items of historical and historical value. The transportation of remains was possible without a permit up to a distance of 30 kilometers. In cases of greater distances, the consent of the district general administration was necessary. Exhumations were also possible.

A decree supplemented the law on burials; this was in regard to burying the dead and ascertaining the cause of death (Ordinance of the Minister of Social Welfare of 30 November 1933). It contained detailed regulations on the ascertainment and documentation of death as well as the persons authorized to do so, the location of cemeteries and the technical and organizational requirements for their establishment and operation, the requirements relating to burial and gravestones, and the transportation of remains and exhumation.

Separate regulations were developed for war graves and cemeteries. A law passed in 1933, and still in force today, was dedicated to them (Act of 28 March 1933). The law indicates what types of graves and cemeteries are recognized as war graves and, at the same time, stipulates the obligation to care for them and treat them with respect. It identifies the bodies responsible for these tasks (Ordinance of the Minister of Internal Affairs of 23 October 1936). The Act describes the rules for granting subsidies for the care of war graves and cemeteries.

Another legal act concerning cemeteries was the current Law on Cemeteries and Burial of the Dead of 1959. The provisions and the regulations resulting from its implementation will be analyzed later.

The most recent legal Act concerning burials is the Act on graves of veterans fighting for freedom and independence in Poland (Act of 22 November 2018).

History of the Funeral Industry

Polish undertakers began to form their facilities, as elsewhere in Europe, in the second half of the 19th century. From newspaper advertisements, telephone directories, address books, and family heirlooms, it can be concluded that funeral parlors started to develop mainly in cities, e.g., in Łódź, Warsaw, Gdynia, Gniezno, Bydgoszcz, Kielce, and Pułtusk.

They were family businesses, training successors in the next generation. Their services included the production of metal and wooden coffins, sale of posthumous underwear, making decorations in mourning houses, transport of corpses with their own horse-drawn hearses, exhumations, purchase of monuments and gravestones – and maintenance of graves in cemeteries. The owners of a carpenter's shop held the title of master carpenter. In 1912, there were already 30 such companies in Warsaw.

At the beginning of the 20th century, these were already modern workshops, adapted to the needs of the varied expectations and abilities of the bourgeoisie (Dąbrowska 2006; Danecka 2004).

During the German occupation, some factories continued to function, albeit unofficially. Others were taken over by German administrators, while their owners worked there as hired staff.

After World War II, the surviving family members of the plants renewed their activities by training the new generation. They also carried out numerous exhumations after the war. There was a change in the model of funeral organization. Municipal funeral companies were established on the remains of Polish and 'post-German' companies. They existed in the framework of state enterprises administering established communal cemeteries, as well as managing municipal green areas and providing other services in the urban space.

During the communist period, plants were taken over by the state, e.g., as "post-German property." If a company managed to keep its funeral home, it was charged a fee for taking over post-German property and was forced to buy it back from the state. In this way, most private funeral homes were destroyed. Nationalization in 1949 was followed by a wave of harassment. The facilities were nationalized and all assets were seized. After the "Thaw" of October 1956 it was possible to open carpenter's workshops again. However, the state created difficulties in the form of bureaucracy (requiring a permit to run a facility), the lack of licensing to transport corpses, numerous inspections, and the rationing of materials for coffin production. In the 1980s there was an opening for the development of crafts. Private funeral parlors began to emerge, but state-owned, communal establishments still dominated.

Since the early 1990s, the free market has been developing in Poland, and the political and economic changes have influenced funerary practices. During the transformation of the 90s, the development of private funeral homes filled the gap in funeral services because undertakers had been traveling to Western Europe and the US to learn the modern management of funeral parlors. The professionalization and specialization of the commercial business began.

At the same time, the beginning of capitalism in Poland created many difficulties, such as a lack of investment capital for starting businesses, economic and criminal problems in the funeral market stemming from 'wild capitalism,' and pathologies in the relations between hospitals and funeral enterprises.

History of Cremation in Poland

In Poland during the interwar period, there was a free-thinking movement demanding the construction of crematoria, but despite the numerous demands (along with the creation of communal cemeteries), these initiatives did not change burial practice (Krzywobłocka 1986, 180). Crematoria built in the first half of the 20th century in German-occupied areas in Gdańsk, Wrocław, Szczecin, Jelenia Góra, Zielona Góra, and Opole were intended for the Protestant German population and were subsequently demolished after the war (Gajewska 2009, 185–198). The ovens that were built in concentration camps during the war differed both in architecture and, as part of the extermination policy, were devoid of ritual symbolism and functioned as death factories. During the communist era, despite the ideology and encouragement of secular burials, no crematorium was built, and so cremations were carried out only in crematoria at medical universities (Gajewska 2009, 207).

Cremation in Poland began much later than in other European countries due to the resistance of the Catholic Church. The first crematorium was opened in Poznań in 1993. However, it was not until the "Letter of the Polish Episcopate on Cremation" published in October 2011 that the number of cremations increased significantly. We read there:

> The Church permits cremation, <if it does not undermine faith in the resurrection of the body> (CCC 2301, CPC can. 1176 §3). However, the Church continues to recommend and support the biblical custom of burying the bodies of the dead.[2]

So it was not a full acceptance of cremation. The letter further reads: "The Church continues to recommend the preservation of the existing custom of burying the bodies of the dead". The Church placed conditions on its approval of cremation, including the recommendation of Mass before cremation, except:

> when someone's death occurred far from the place of residence and cremation makes it easier to bring the mortal remains of the deceased, and also when the funeral attendees come from far away and it is difficult for them to be at the two parts of the funeral, that is, at the Mass combined with the last farewell to the body of the deceased and, after some time, the rite of placing the urn in the grave or columbarium.

The Episcopate has also opposed the scattering of ashes advocating that the urn be buried only in a cemetery in a grave – or in a columbarium.

With the growth of private crematoria, the number of cremations continues to increase. The factors influencing the increase in the number of cremations are the lower funeral allowance (the price of a cremation funeral is generally lower, although there are many factors involved, such as transport to the crematory), the increasing number of crematoria, the popularization of cremation by some business owners, the increasing number of exhumations for burial in a single grave, the number of the cremations of stillborn babies and deceased newborns, the possibility of keeping an urn in a family grave, the decreasing number of cemetery spaces and their price, and sanitary reasons in the case of infectious diseases. In 2002, the Regional Association of Cremation Supporters was formed to promote the idea of cremation.

Historic Development of Cemeteries

The genesis of modern Polish cemeteries is directly related to Christianity and the late Middle Ages, when Polish statehood began to take shape. The temple and its surroundings were considered by Christians as the most noble burial place. It was believed that by being buried in the shadow of a temple, the dead would be able to "experience the salutary influence of holiness emanating from the House of God" (Majdecka-Strzeżek 2016, 24). In the late Middle Ages (12th–13th centuries), the Dominican, Carmelite, Franciscan, and Benedictine orders became widespread, as well as small cemeteries established by the monks and dedicated to them, which were an important element of the monastic garden layout (Majdecki 2008). At the end of the 12th century, settlers of Jewish origin began arriving in Poland from Western Europe, as evidenced by the Jewish cemeteries scattered throughout the historical areas of the Republic, including the oldest and the most important in all of Europe: the Remuh cemetery in Krakow from 1533, the pre-1541 cemetery in Lublin, the pre-1545 cemetery in Szczebrzeszyn, and the pre-1548 cemetery in Lesko.

As stated by Kolbuszewski (1996) and Rudkowski (2003) the network of church cemeteries was formed in Poland around the 13th century and for the next five centuries, until the turn of the 18th century, not much changed in them. However, in the mid-18th century, the discussions about the need to improve the hygienic condition of European cities began, and the ceremonial dedication of the first "extra muros" cemetery in Poland (so-called Świętokrzyski Cemetery) took place on 1783 (Mórawski 1989). Instead of using this new cemetery space, burials continued in overcrowded church cemeteries. Prejudice was broken only by the funeral of the Smolensk bishop, Gabriel Wodziński in 1788.

He instructed in his will that he be buried in Świętokrzyski Cemetery. This event inaugurated the action of relocating cemeteries in the Polish lands. It was the beginning of a new chapter in the history of cemetery design. The first laws on cemeteries were already issued during the partitions: a decree of Emperor Frederick of 1773 (for Polish lands annexed to the Prussian partition), a court decree of Emperor Joseph II of 1784 (for Polish lands included in the Austrian partition) and a decree of Tsar Alexander I of 1817 (for Polish lands in the Russian partition). Localization and shaping of cemetery layout were processed in a similar way as in Western European countries (Ariès 1982). The legislators required that necropolises be established away from settlement units, in dry areas not prone to flooding. The following cemeteries were established then: Plock (1780), Ostrow Wielkopolski (1782), Tarnow (1790), Powązki cemetery in Warsaw (1790), Rzeszów (1792), the old Podgorski cemetery in Krakow (1794), Lipowa Street in Lublin (1794), Rakowicki cemetery in Krakow (1803), and the Cemetery of Eminent Greater Poland Citizens in Poznan (1808). A cemetery became a public park and a museum in one. As Anna Majdecka-Strzeżek noted (2016, 39), "natural irregular compositions were valued where the relationship between the deceased and nature was especially accentuated." In the 19th century, cultural tourism flourished and cemeteries became objects of interest to travelers. Père Lachaise, for example, was from the beginning listed in guidebooks as one of Paris's peculiarities. In addition, gardening guides such as "Miscellaneous Thoughts on How to Set Up gardens" by Izabela Czartoryska (1805) promoted the image of the cemetery as a garden and park. In the face of these messages – ambitions began to increase among the managers of Polish cemeteries so that Polish sites could also aspire to great works of cemetery art (Lewandowski 1939).

After Poland lost its independence, a patriotic theme also became apparent in cemeteries. In a society living under the partitions, cemeteries – with the graves of heroes meritorious to the cause of independence – gained a kind of sanctity. The funerals of prominent Poles repeatedly provided an opportunity to manifest patriotic feelings. Hence the care for the appearance of cemeteries, especially since the second half of the 19th century (Janiszewska-Jakubiak 2020).

It should be emphasized that subjection to different jurisdictions also impinged on the diversity of types of cemeteries or their aesthetics. Thus, in the territory of the Prussian partition in the 19th century, family cemeteries began to take shape. This trend continued until the early 20th century. Family cemeteries were located within parks or in close proximity to the estate (Majdecka-Strzeżek 2016). The universality of family cemeteries became a characteristic element, inscribing these objects permanently in the historical landscape of Mazury, Silesia, or Greater Poland.

WWII was a clear caesura in the history of Polish cemeteries, as a large number of facilities were destroyed then. Postwar repercussions in the form of a change of borders (as a result of the Potsdam Agreement from 1945, Poland lost 179000 square kilometres, 45% of prewar territories in the east) and displacement of the population impacted the condition of cemeteries – many civilian and military sites were deprived of permanent care. Necropolises in the former eastern territories of the multinational and multicultural Republic remained outside the Polish borders (Janiszewska-Jakubiak 2020). In 1944–1989 Poland was a non-sovereign state under the political domination of the ZSRR. In 1945–1958, intensive efforts were made to close post-German cemeteries in the so-called Western and Northern Territories. Local administrative bodies were given extensive prerogatives to establish municipal cemeteries and to liquidate religious facilities (Rogowska 2014, Stachowiak 2015).

In the 1980s, a nationwide campaign to inventory cemeteries and cemetery sites was inaugurated, creating an opportunity to restore the history and knowledge of cemeteries established before 1945 (Burak, Okólska 2007).

Nowadays, irrational use of cemetery space and intensification of historical cemetery development lead to the degradation of cemetery composition. Due to this, cremation is gaining popularity in Poland. It helps to alleviate the problem of overcrowded and unsightly cemeteries, which cause a lot of trouble, especially for the authorities of large cities (Długozima 2020).

Notes

1 According to the Polish Language Dictionary (1968, 1395), 'Żalnik' is a pagan cemetery, but also a grave, a barrow, and an urn with the ashes of the deceased.
2 "List Episkopatu Polski w sprawie kremacji" (Letter of the Polish Episcopate on cremation). http://www.opoka.org.pl/aktualnosci/news.php?id=40254&s= opoka [21.11.2012].

References

Act of 17 March 1932 on the burial of the dead and ascertaining the cause of death (JoL of 1932 No.35 item.359)
Act of 22 November 2018 on graves of veterans fighting for freedom and independence of Poland (JoL of 2018, item.2529).
Ariès Philippe 1982, *The Hour of Our Death. The Classic History of Western Attitudes Towards Death Over the Last One Thousand Years*, Oxford University Press, Oxford
Basic Sanitary Act of 19 July 1919 (JoL of 1919, 9No.63 item.371).
Biegeleisen Henryk 1930, *Śmierć w obrzędach, zwyczajach i wierzeniach ludu polskiego* (Death in the rites, customs, and beliefs of the Polish people), Dom Książki Polskiej, Warszawa

Burak Marek, Okólska Hanna 2007, *Cmentarze dawnego Wrocławia* (Cemeteries of old Wrocław), Muzeum Architektury we Wrocławiu, Wrocław

Concordat between the Holy See and the Republic of Poland, signed in Rome on 10 February 1925 (ratified in accordance with the Act of 23 April 1925, JoL. of 1925. No.47, item 324). (JoL of 1925 No.72, item.501)

Czartoryska Izabela 1805, *Myśli różne o sposobie zakładania ogrodów* (Miscellaneous thoughts on how to establish gardens), Wilhelm Bogumił Korn print, Wrocław

Chróścicki Juliusz A. 1974, *Pompa Funebris. Z dziejów kultury staropolskiej, (Pompa Funebris.* From the history of Old Polish culture), PWN, Warszawa

Danecka Aleksandra 2004, "Zakłady pogrzebowe w przedwojennej Warszawie" (Funeral homes in pre-war Warsaw), *Memento* 1, 15

Dziobek-Romański Jacek, 1998, Cemeteries – outline of historical, legal and canonical regulations [in:] "Rocznik Historyczno-Archiwalny", T. XIII, Przemyśl, pp. 3–32.

Dąbrowska Joanna 2006, *Charakterystyka cmentarzy i usług pogrzebowych na terenie Gdyni w latach 1920–1939* (Characteristics of cemeteries and funeral services in Gdynia between 1920–1939), Master Thesis, University of Gdansk

Długozima Anna 2020, "How might landscapes be better designed to accommodate increasing cremation practices in Europe?" Vol. 87, *Landscape Online*, 1–31

Fisher Adam 1921, *Zwyczaje pogrzebowe ludu polskiego* (Funeral customs of the Polish people), Zakład Narodowy im. Ossolińskich, Lwów

Gajewska Magdalena 2009, *Prochy i Diamenty. Kremacja ciała zmarłego człowieka jako zjawisko społeczne i kulturowe* (Ashes and Diamonds. Cremation of the body of a dead person as a social and cultural phenomenon), Nomos, Kraków

Janiszewska-Jakubiak Dorota 2020, "Zachować pamięć" (Preserve the memory) (in:) Czyż A. S., Gutowski B. (eds) *Podręcznik do inwentaryzacji polskich cmentarzy i nagrobków poza granicami kraju* (Manual for the inventory of Polish cemeteries and tombstones abroad), Wydawnictwo Polonika, Warszawa, 3–8

Kolbuszewski Jacek 1996, *Cmentarze* (Cemeteries), Wydawnictwo Dolnośląskie, Wrocław

Krzywobłocka Bożena 1986, *Stare i nowe obyczaje* (Old and new customs), IWZZ, Warszawa

Kubiak Anna E. 2015, *Pogrzeby to nasze życie* (Funerals are our lives), IFiS PAN, Warszawa

"List Episkopatu Polski w sprawie kremacji" (Letter of the Polish Episcopate on cremation). http://www.opoka.org.pl/aktualnosci/news.php?id=40254&s= opoka [21.11.2012].

Łuka Alicja 1956, *Kultura Pomorska na Pomorzu Wschodnim* (Pomeranian Culture in Eastern Pomerania), Muzeum Pomorskie, Gdańsk

Lewandowski Henryk 1939, "O większą kulturę w cmentarnictwie. Z rozważań i doświadczeń przy zakładaniu cmentarzy" (For More Culture in Cemeteries. From Cemetery Establishment Considerations and Experiences), Teologia Praktyczna, Vol. 1–3, 225–236

Majdecka-Strzeżek Anna 2016, "Ogrody wiecznej pamięci w krajobrazie kulturowym" (Memorial gardens in the cultural landscape), *Kwartalnik Architektury i Urbanistyki*, No. 3, 23–36

14   *Anna E. Kubiak et al.*

Majdecki Longin 2008, *Historia ogrodów* (Gardens history), PWN, Warszawa
Ordinance of the Minister of Internal Affairs of 23 October 1936 issued in agreement with the Ministers of Military Affairs and Social Welfare on the implementation of the Act of 28 March 1933 on war graves and cemeteries (JoL No.85, item.595).
Mórawski Kazimierz 1989, Przewodnik historyczny po cmentarzach warszawskich (Historical Guide to Warsaw Cemeteries), Wydawnictwo PTTK "Kraj", Warszawa
Ordinance of the Minister of Social Welfare of 30 November 1933 on the burial of the dead and ascertaining the cause of death, issued in agreement with the Minister of the Interior and the Minister of Religious Denominations and Public Enlightenment. https://sip.lex.pl/#/act/16836594/86666/chowanie-zmarlych-i-stwierdzanie-przyczyny-zgonu?cm=RELATIONS.
Ordinance of the Ministry of Public Health of 6 May 1920 on the transportation and exhumation of corpses (JoL of 1920 No.42, item.257).
Rogowska Barbara 2014, "Stanowisko władz komunistycznych w latach siedemdziesiątych XX wieku w zakresie cmentarnictwa wyznaniowego i komunalnego" (The position of the communist regime on the religious and communal cemeteries in the 1970s.), *Annales Universitatis Paedagogicae Cracoviensis Studia Politologica*, XIII, Folia 165, 75–93
Rudkowski Tadeusz 2003, "Jak wyprowadzono cmentarze z miast polskich na przełomie XVIII i XIX wieku" (How cemeteries were moved out of Polish cities at the turn of the 18th and 19th centuries) [in:] *Studium Urbis Charisteria Teresiae Zarębska Anno Iubilaei Oblata*, Wydawnictwo Książkowe "Linia", Gdańsk, 189–194
Stachowiak Andrzej 2015, "Niemieckie cmentarze na Ziemiach Zachodnich jako miejsca niepamięci" (German Cemeteries in the Western Lands as the Places of Oblivion), *Prace Etnograficzne*, 43 (2), 123–140

3 Mortality

Piotr Szukalski

General Characteristics of Mortality in Poland

The Number of Deaths

Over the last three decades, the number of deaths was generally quite stable despite the progressive ageing of the population, leading to an expected increase in the number of the deceased. The appearance of Covid-19 significantly modified the situation, as there were 477,400 deaths in 2020, while in 2021 there were 519,500, compared with a 50-year annual average death rate of 394,900 and 365,200 (GUS 2014). However, it is worth noting that the difference *in minus* between the expectations and the evolution of the mortality rate started growing already in 2015. While in 1992–2015, population ageing was compensated for by improving health, which is most frequently synthetically described as newborn life expectancy, the last years before Covid-19 indicated a period of stagnation or even a small increase in the mortality rate. The greatest increase in the mortality rate was recorded among men aged 60–80 years and women aged 65–90 years (Wróblewska 2019). In consequence, between 2014 and 2019, the life expectancy of men increased by only 0.3 years and by 0.2 years in the case of women, while the earlier average annual increase was 0.25–0.3 per year.

The first two years of the Covid-19 epidemic shortened newborn life expectancy for men by 2.3 years and by 2.1 years for women, which means that in 2021 this synthetic measure reached values observed 8–10 years earlier. The recorded scale of the increase in mortality and over-mortality rates (i.e., compared with the average rates from the years 2016–2019) in Poland was one of the highest in Europe[1] (Figure 3.1).

Age Structure of the Deceased

The last decades also saw a considerable change in the distribution of deaths by age, as there was an increase in the significance of deaths over 70 or even 80 years of age (see Figure 3.2). On the one hand, this was a result of a reduced mortality rate, meaning that more and more people

DOI: 10.4324/9781003207634-3

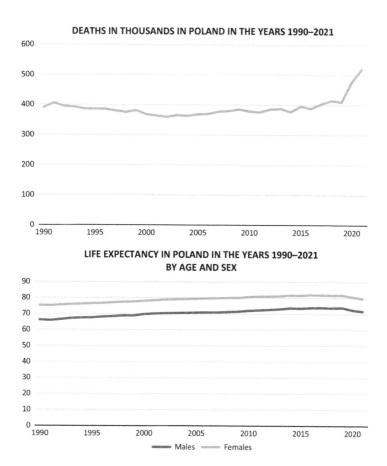

Figure 3.1 Deaths and life expectancy in Poland in the years 1990–2021.

Source: Database, Statistics Poland, and author's own calculations, https://demografia.stat.gov.pl/bazademografia/TrwanieZycia.aspx.

reached an advanced age, and on the other hand it was a consequence of a change in the age structure of the population, with an increasing share of old and very old people.

The Marital Status of the Deceased

The marital status of the population of dying people changes. For both sexes, the share of married people decreases, while the share of widows and widowers increases (Table 3.1).

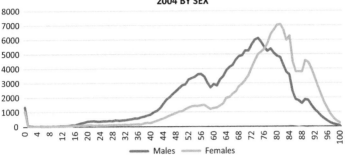

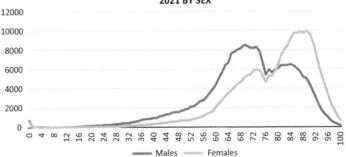

Figure 3.2 The distribution of deaths in one-year age groups in 2004 and 2021 by sex.

Source: Database, Statistics Poland, and the author's own calculations, https://demografia.stat.gov.pl/bazademografia/TrwanieZycia.aspx.

Table 3.1 The marital status of the deceased in the years 1990–2021 by sex (as a percentage of the total number of deaths of people of a given sex)

Marital status	Males				Females			
	1990	2000	2010	2021	1990	2000	2010	2021
Married	66.3	64.1	58.7	56.2	26.7	25.4	23.8	22.7
Unmarried	10.0	11.3	13.5	14.4	9.8	8.7	7.4	6.8
Widows, widowers	17.9	18.1	18.5	19.0	60.1	61.5	62.6	61.9
Divorcees	5.7	6.5	9.0	10.3	3.4	4.4	6.0	8.6

Source: Database, Statistics Poland, and author's own calculations, https://demografia.stat.gov.pl/bazademografia/TrwanieZycia.aspx.

The marital status of the deceased is closely related to their age and sex. While it is generally easy – considering the typical chronological order of events starting and ending life together – to explain the relationship between age and marital status, it should be strongly emphasised that in the case of women, the effect of widowhood is definitely greater as a result of not only male over-mortality but also a typical age difference (in the case of approx. two-thirds of Polish marriages, men are older than their wives).

Places of Death

Polish statistics allow us to identify the place of death, defined as a hospital, a different healthcare facility (a hospice, a permanent care centre, a nursing home), the home (the place where the deceased lived), and other places. In the long term, one can see the so-called medicalisation of death, which means that the care of individuals in their last days, weeks, or months is entrusted to specialist healthcare institutions. Due to the medicalisation of death, more and more deaths take place in healthcare institutions. This process has also been observed over the last 50 years in Poland (Szukalski 2021) as, instead of slightly more than one-third of all deaths in healthcare facilities in 1970, there were nearly 60% of such deaths in 2019 (Table 3.2).

The Covid-19 pandemic changed these long-term trends. As many hospitals were turned into facilities taking care of epidemic victims and many elective surgeries were rescheduled, there were definitely more deaths at home, which was an indirect result of the above limitations. Most probably, these changes are temporary and, after the situation from before the pandemic is restored, the previous trend will continue.

Table 3.2 The distribution of deaths by place of death in Poland in the years 1990–2021 (as a percentage of all deaths)[2]

Year	Number of deaths	% of deaths			
		Hospital	*Other medical institution*	*Home*	*Other*
1990	390,343	46.6	1.5	45.2	6.2
2000	368,028	50.1	3.0	40.9	6.0
2010	378,478	50.2	6.2	37.8	5.8
2019	409,709	50.8	8.3	35.3	5.6
2020	477,355	47.8	7.6	39.3	5.3
2021	519,517	52.2	6.5	36.8	4.5

Source: Own calculations based on Roczniki Demograficzne GUS (Demographic Yearbooks of GUS) – 2006: 376; 2016: 366, and data from the Database, Statistics Poland.

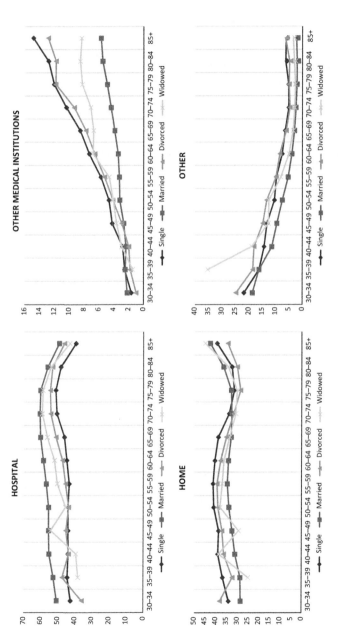

Figure 3.3 The place of death by age and marital status of the deceased in 2021 (as a percentage of the total number of deaths at a given age and with a given marital status).

Source: Database, Statistics Poland, and own calculations, https://demografia.stat.gov.pl/bazademografia/TrwanieZycia.aspx.

What should also be emphasised is the relatively low (compared with Europe) share of people dying in other medical institutions, which reflects the very low (compared with the UE) share of seniors living in residential care facilities.

As can be inferred, an important factor determining the place of illness and death – through access to care ensured by closest relatives, mostly one's spouse – is marital status. The D database of Statistics Poland allows the generation of appropriate data, however, without considering sex. Analysing only the deceased over 30 years of age, meaning those whose numbers are high enough (in the case of widows and widowers, there are no people aged 30–34 years who died in some categories of places), to generate appropriate data, one can see considerable differences in the distribution of deaths by their place (Figure 3.3).

Causes of Death

Poland faces a problem with determining the exact cause of death, which is reflected by, among other things, a large share of insufficiently determined and unknown causes (so-called garbage codes). This group of deaths constitutes the third most important cause of death, reaching particularly high values in the case of the oldest people. As a consequence, WHO has not considered data from Poland in their databases since the beginning of 2014.

Generally, in the period analysed, one can see a decrease in the number of deaths caused by cardiovascular diseases (which is attributed to more effective methods of treating hypertension) and a slow increase in the number of deaths caused by respiratory diseases, but mostly tumours (Table 3.3).

The above causes differ depending on age. The presented data for women (see Figure 3.4) and men (see Figure 3.5) clearly indicate that – even during the Covid-19 pandemic – as we analyse older and older groups, the significance of cardiovascular and respiratory diseases permanently grows. Whereas in the case of tumours, the maximum

Table 3.3 Causes of death in the years 1990–2021

Cause	1990	2000	2010	2019	2020	2021
Cardiovascular diseases	53.4	47.7	46.0	39.4	36.6	34.8
Tumours	19.1	23.4	25.4	26.5	22.8	19.6
Accidents, injuries, and poisoning	7.8	7.0	6.2	4.9	4.2	4.2
Respiratory diseases	4.0	5.0	5.1	6.6	6.0	5.4
Infectious and parasitic diseases	0.8	0.6	0.7	0.4	0.3	0.4
Covid-19	-	-	-	-	8.7	17.9

Source: Database, Statistics Poland, and own calculations, https://demografia.stat.gov.pl/bazademografia/TrwanieZycia.aspx.

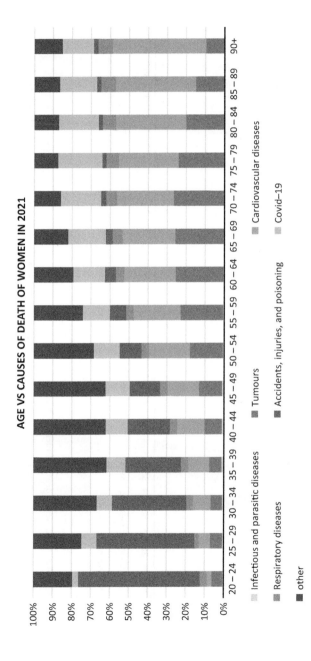

Figure 3.4 Age vs causes of death of women in 2021.

Source: Database, Statistics Poland, and own calculations, https://demografia.stat.gov.pl/bazademografia/Tables.aspx.

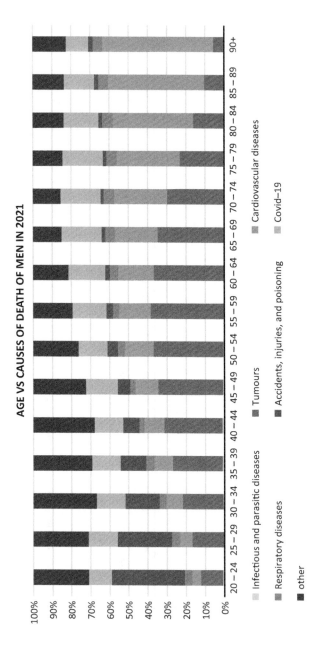

Figure 3.5. Age vs causes of death of men in 2021.

Source: Database, Statistics Poland, and own calculations, https://demografia.stat.gov.pl/bazademografia/Tables.aspx.

percentage is observed among women aged 55–64 years, while in the case of men – at the age of 60–74 years. The above regularities, however, should be treated as probable and not certain on account of the already mentioned significance of garbage codes, which increases with each age group.

Spatial Differentiation of the Mortality Rate

Contemporary Poland is still a country with considerable differentiation of the mortality rate in spatial terms. Generally, the lowest mortality rate measured with the already mentioned life expectancy is typical of the largest cities, mostly thanks to a better social structure (education, high quality of workplace, high remuneration and, indirectly, pension), and the population living in the southern and eastern parts of the country (a population that is traditional in cultural terms, and religious) with overrepresentation of inhabitants of the country and small towns.

The worst situation was identified in post-industrial areas and territories incorporated into Poland after the Second World War, where the level of long-term residency (living in the same place from birth) is much lower, and social and family ties are much weaker.

Notes

1 https://ec.europa.eu/eurostat/databrowser/view/DEMO_R_MWK_TS__custom_
2011619/bookmark/table?lang=en&bookmarkId=a222c8d9-99f7-4845-a3d1-
7c63e35c2d21 [01.02.2023].
2 GUS 2022.

References

GUS 2014, "Prognoza ludności" (Population forecast). Prognoza ludności - Baza Demografia - Główny Urząd Statystyczny [04.02.2023].
GUS 2022. Główny Urząd Statystyczny / Obszary tematyczne / Roczniki statystyczne / Roczniki Statystyczne / Rocznik Demograficzny 2022 [04.02.2023].
Szukalski Piotr 2021, "Czy Covid-19 wpłynął na zmianę miejsca zgonu Polaków?" (Did Covid-19 affect the change in the place of death of Poles?), *Demografia i Gerontologia Społeczna. Biuletyn Informacyjny*, No. 1, http://hdl.handle.net/11089/37729 [01.02.2023].
Wróblewska Wiktoria 2019, "Zmiana liczby zgonów i trwania życia w latach 2016–2018. Przyczynek do analizy zgonów w Polsce" (Change in deaths and life expectancy from 2016 to 2018. A contribution to the analysis of deaths in Poland), *Studia Demograficzne*, No. 1(175), 9–25. 10.33119/SD.2019.1.1 [01.02.2023].

4 Legal Framework of Funerals and Cemeteries

*Agnieszka Wedeł-Domaradzka and
Anna Długozima*

Law and Regulations Concerning Funerary Activity

The current law on cemeteries and burial is the Act on Cemeteries and Burial of the Dead of 1959. The document has been subject to more than 20 amendments over the years (the most recent took effect on January 1, 2023). However, despite its numerous updates, it still does not provide for its more modern forms. Two drafts of a new law on cemeteries – one from the government and one from the citizens – are under consideration.

Separate regulations are provided for graves and war cemeteries. In this respect, one of the oldest legal regulations, the Act of 1933 on War Graves and Cemeteries, is still in force (Act of 28 March 1933).

Registering Death

According to the Polish legislature, all deaths are subject to registration. Further, the law stipulates that deaths shall be registered at the competent registry office closest to where the death took place or where the corpse was found (Article 16, Act of 28 November 2014).

The entities obliged to report a death are the same persons who are entitled to perform a burial (Article 10(1) of the Act of 31 January 1959). In specific cases, the notifiers may be other entities.

The head shall notify the municipal representative of the facility or unit of the municipality having jurisdiction over the place of death of a person of undetermined identity residing in a medical facility or a social welfare organizational unit, and if the public prosecutor or the police find the body in a condition or in circumstances that make its identification impossible. In such cases, the notification is intended to ensure that the task of registering the death is accomplished.

The procedure for declaring a death involves submitting a death certificate to the head of the registry office within three days of the date of the death. However, where death has occurred as a result of infectious

DOI: 10.4324/9781003207634-4

disease, the notification shall be made within 24 hours of death (Article 93, Act of 28 November 2014).

The manager supplements the death certificate submitted to him with an annotation that the death has been registered in the civil registry or with an annotation that the death has been reported if, due to the unavailability of the registry, it is not possible to register the death on the day it was reported. It is also incumbent on the body to which the death certificate has been issued to forward part of it to the cemetery administration for the burial of the body (Article 11(4a) and (4b) of the Act of 31 January 1959).[1]

The declaration of death is documented in the form of a protocol. This protocol is signed by the person who reports the death and the head of the civil registry office. The content of the protocol is regulated by law and includes the primary identification data of the deceased. These data include the deceased's surname, family name, forename(s), date and place of birth, marital status, nationality, and PESEL number, if known to the declarant of death; the date, time and place of death or, if unknown, the date, time and place where the corpse was found; the surnames, family names, forenames of the parents of the deceased, if known; the surname, surname at birth, forename(s) and PESEL number of the deceased's spouse, if known, if married at the time of death; the surname and forename(s) or name of the declarant of death; the surname and forename of the expert or translator if s/he took part in the act; the surname and forename of the head of the registered office receiving the registration; the year of marriage of the parents of a deceased child, the date of birth of the mother of the deceased child in the event of the death of a child under one year of age (Article 94, Act of 28 November 2014. Law on civil status records).

Once the death has been registered, a death certificate is drawn up. It should be drawn up on the day of the death registration. The documents necessary for the declaration of death are the death certificate and the death report. The death certificate drawn up by the authorities of the competent municipality contains similar data to the declaration of death.

A reasonable suspicion that the cause of death was a crime creates an obligation on the part of the physician or another person appointed to inspect the corpse to notify the competent public prosecutor or the nearest police station immediately. If a crime is suspected, the burial of the corpse will require permission from the public prosecutor in addition to the death certificate.

Separate regulations are provided for situations where a death certificate is drawn up for a person of undetermined identity. In such cases, it is necessary to include the date, time, and place of death, the date and time as well as the place and circumstances under which the corpse was found, the sex and presumed age of the deceased, a description of the external appearance of the corpse, a description of clothes and other objects found on the deceased, designation of the police unit or indication of the public prosecutor if notification is made that the corpse has been found in a condition or circumstances which prevent its identification, or designation of the medical facility or social welfare unit. If, in the course of further operations, the identity of the deceased has been ascertained by those carrying out identification operations before the death certificate has been drawn up, the head of the civil registry office shall be notified to draw up a new death certificate containing a note to the effect that this certificate replaces the existing one, which shall not be disclosed. Where the drawing up of a death certificate is the result of a court ruling acknowledging or declaring death, the death certificate should also contain a note indicating the court issuing the ruling and the file reference number of the case.

Among the peculiar legal solutions is the registration of stillbirth. Polish law does not treat this situation equally to death since a stillborn child could not die as a natural person, as it has not acquired legal subjectivity (Sierpowska 2020). Consequently, a death certificate is not drawn up, but only an annotation of stillbirth is entered in the birth certificate.

The registration of a death occurring on board a Polish sea or airship, warship, or military aircraft is considered a unique situation for the registration of death. In such a case, the master shall document in the form of a protocol confirming the death, specifying the place of death in this protocol.

Body Transportation and Repatriation

The transport of corpses and remains and the procedures for their return are regulated by the Law on Cemeteries and Burying of the Dead, and its executive regulation (Ordinance of the MZ of 27 December 2007 and Ordinance of the MZ of 7 December 2001). According to the law (Article 14 of the Act of 31 January 1959), the transport of corpses and remains may be carried out by rail, airplane, and ships within the borders of the RP, and outside the borders of the RP, in the case where the death occurred on the territory of the RP. The condition for such transport is to obtain a permit from the competent state district sanitary inspector. When the situation of transport relates to corpses and remains outside the borders of the RP, the permission for transport is issued upon submission of the required documents to the competent authority of the state on whose territory they are to be buried, as well as the states through whose territory they are to be transported, stating that there are no obstacles to the burial or importation of the corpse or remains on the territory of a given state. A situation is also allowed in which the transport of the corpse and remains through the territory of the RP will take place after obtaining a certificate issued by the Polish consul in the country where the transport is to take place. This certificate should state that there are no obstacles to bringing the corpse and remains into the territory of another state.

In order to bring the corpse and remains from abroad for burial, it is necessary to obtain a permit from the starost competent for where the corpse and remains are to be buried. This permit is issued after consultation with the competent state district sanitary inspector. The second document, necessary for the purposes mentioned above, is a certificate from the Polish consul, issued upon presentation of the permit from the starost, stating that the corpse and remains may be brought to the territory of the RP. The persons who can apply for the indicated permits and certificates are those authorized by the legislature to perform the burial. The deadlines for issuing these documents are relatively short and amount to three days from the date of applying for the permit or certificate.

The exceptions to this are situations where the death has occurred due to a contagious disease listed in a list maintained by the Minister responsible for health. In such a case, transport permits and permits to bring in the corpse shall not be issued until two years have elapsed from the date of death. The regulations require that transport be carried out in compliance with conditions ensuring proper sanitary and technical safety of transport. Detailed regulations on transport are laid down in a decree issued by the Minister in charge of health matters in agreement with the Minister in charge of foreign affairs (Ordinance of the MZ of 27 December 2007). Following the content of this Regulation, in order to transport human remains and corpses, a relevant application should be submitted, including the identification data of the applicant and the data of the person whose remains or corpses the application concerns. In addition, the application must be accompanied by a death certificate or another official document confirming death and the documents required by the State on whose territory the corpse or remains are to be buried or through whose territory their transport is to take place. The Ordinance also provides for the technical and sanitary conditions to be met through road transport intended to transport bodies and human remains (§4 Ordinance of the MZ of 27 December 2007).

Legal Framework and Practice of Burial and Exhumation

The matter of the right to burial is determined by Article 10 of the Act on Cemeteries and Burial of the Deceased. According to the regulation provided for therein, the right to bury the body is vested in the closest family of the deceased. A person who voluntarily undertakes to do so also has the right of burial. The law provides for an order of priority for persons entitled to bury the body, with the right to bury a person's body being granted to the next-best-ranking person only if there is no next-best-ranking person or if the next-best-ranking person is unwilling or unable to exercise his or her right (Judgment of the SN of 25 September 1972; Judgment of the SN of 11 November 1976). Special regulations apply to the burial of military persons who have died in active military service, in respect of whom the competent military authorities exercise this right of burial following military regulations. The second group whose burial is regulated especially are persons of merit to the state and society. Their burial right is exercised by state bodies, institutions, and social organizations (Wedeł-Domaradzka 2021).

The jurisprudence also contains the position that this provision does not determine priority but only states who has the right (Judgment of the SN of 7 June 1966), as well as the position indicating that the order provided for in Article 10 is relevant; however, "the factual circum-stances of the case, and in particular, the relationship of the deceased prior to death with the various persons mentioned in this provision, as well as his expressed will as to the place and type of burial be in favor of giving priority to the rights of other members of the family than those who are mentioned in the provision in the first place" (Judgment of the SN of 23 May 1975). In the event of a dispute, the court will examine the relationship between the deceased and those entitled to burial and may consider it desirable, from the perspective of principles of social con-science, to grant legal protection to the personal welfare of those with a right to burial further down the line (Księżak, Robaczyński 2012).

It should be stressed that the question of the will of the deceased person as to the place and manner of burial is also significant. Admittedly, although the deceased person no longer has the legal capacity, nor are his or her rights protected, it must be recognized that the will of the deceased is nevertheless more than a moral imperative (Judgment of the SN of 6 November 1978).

The issue of the exhumation of corpses is compassionate precisely because of its impact on the right to the veneration of the deceased. This right, due to its protection under the provisions on the protection of personal rights (Articles 23 and 24 of the Act of 23 April 1964), is granted to a broader catalog of entities than relatives and relations. An extension of this catalog is the possibility for the right of veneration to arise for a person who has voluntarily undertaken to perform the burial. The catalog of entities that may request an exhumation is limited to the catalog of persons entitled to burial. The request may be made by one of the entitled persons, but the others must give their undoubted consent (Judgment of the NSA of 5 October 2021). The right to request exhumation does not rely on the order provided for persons entitled to perform the burial, which means that the right to worship of any person who was emotionally connected to the deceased and who wishes to perform this worship is protected. Consequently, any person with a right to worship may have an interest in the burial place and, if he considers the exhumation to be in breach of rights, may object to it (Judgment of the SN of 13 January 1965). It is up to the court to determine to what extent this objection can be practical. As the case law indicates (Judgment of the SN of 19 November 2020), there is a possibility of a conflict between the personal rights of the relatives of the deceased. This determines the need to find criteria for their removal. One may be the order of persons entitled to bury the deceased. In typical situations, this order reflects the intensity of the relationship that linked the deceased to his or her relatives. If these relationships were different, this would need to be considered. There are also views according to which one cannot exclude a situation in which a person not mentioned in Article 10 of the UCChZ could be entitled to burial since, as it results from the case law, this provision belongs to the sphere of public law and does not directly regulate the issue of personal rights (Judgment of the SN of 19 November 2020, Judgment of the SN of 31 March 1980). In such a situation it should be considered that such persons could meet the requirement of voluntarily expressing their will to bury the deceased.

The exhumation procedure itself, in relation to the possibility of disturbing the peace of the deceased and their relatives, should be treated as an exceptional event in exceptional circumstances and where there are compelling reasons (Judgment of the SN of 16 June 1998, Judgment of the SN of 29 January 2003 Judgment of the SN of 6 February 2008, Judgment of the SN of 17 February 2016). These include, for example, the only way to allow the authorized person or persons to worship (Judgment of the SN of 19 November 2020). A state health inspector must give consent for exhumation.

The possibility of exhumation is also provided for on the order of the public prosecutor or the court. In the case of a decision on such an exhumation, persons entitled to burial cannot object. Such a legal solution was criticized by the ECtHR, which stated that it is the duty of the Polish authorities to find a balance between the requirements of conducting an effective investigation and respect for private and family life. Thus, although there may be circumstances justifying exhumation despite the objections of the next of kin, they should have the right to avail themselves of a legal remedy protecting them from the total arbitrariness of the prosecutor or the court in this matter (ECtHR, Solska, and Rybicka v. Poland, Nowicki 2019). The possibility of exhumation is related to the change of destination of the land on which the cemetery is located. In such a case, by the decision of the sanitary inspector, the corpse buried in the area whose destination is changed is exhumed and subject to burial in another place.

Exhumation provided in connection with proceedings conducted by the IPN shall be considered a particular type of exhumation (Act of 15 May 2015). Such an exhumation takes place when there is a suspicion, or it has been established that under the existing grave, there is a resting place of a person who lost their life as a result of the fight against the imposed totalitarian system or as a result of totalitarian repressions or ethnic cleansing from 8 November 1917 to 31 July 1990. The prosecutor decides to carry out such an exhumation of the locally competent commission for prosecuting crimes against the Polish Nation. Where it is not possible to bury the body and remains in the same grave, the voivode competent for the location of the grave, at the request of the President of the IPN – Commission for the Prosecution of Crimes against the Polish Nation – issues a decision on the reburial of the body and remains in another grave.

Coroner: A New Vision of Confirming, Documenting, and Registering Death

Polish legal regulations allow for confirmation of death by a physician, senior medical officer, feldsher, and, in certain situations, a midwife (in relation to children) (Ordinance of the MZiOS of 3 August 1961). In practice, however, the pronouncement of death is the domain of medical doctors.

The idea of establishing the institution of a coroner (Article 5, Draft of 21 November 2019) was intended to facilitate the process of ascertaining, documenting, and registering the death. According to the draft, the right to practice this profession is granted to a person who has the right to practice medicine in the territory of the RP; has total legal capacity; has not been convicted of an intentional crime prosecuted by public indictment or a fiscal crime; has a specialization in forensic medicine, pathology, anaesthesiology, and intensive care, emergency medicine or at least three years of work experience in the medical profession and has undergone training in a forensic medicine unit of a medical university. It is also acceptable for a person in the course of specialization in forensic medicine or pathology to become a coroner after completing the second year of specialization training and obtaining the consent of the head of the specialization. A medical doctor conducts the training to become a coroner with a specialization in forensic medicine. The training program shall include at least 30 hours and ends with a certificate of competence. The provincial governor maintains the list of coroners. The task of the coroner is to confirm a death. He or she does this by carrying out specific activities (Article 5, Draft of 21 November 2019). The death certificate must reflect the determination and confirmation of death and the above actions.

If the coroner suspects that a third party may have contributed to the death, or that the death was the result of an accident or suicide, the coroner must immediately notify the public prosecutor or the nearest police unit responsible for the place where the body was discovered. If the coroner determines that the death was due to an infectious disease, shall immediately notify the district sanitary inspector or the state border sanitary inspector competent for where the corpse was discovered. In addition, the coroner's task is to notify the nearest police unit if it is impossible to clearly identify the person whose body is being examined. The coroner also notifies the public prosecutor's office responsible for where the body was discovered or the nearest police unit when called upon to examine the body of a fetus or newborn child.

It is also the coroner's task to draw up a death certificate when the corpse is handed over to a person authorized or obliged to perform the burial.

Procedure for Dealing with Corpses Not Buried by Entitled Persons

In a situation where none of the entitled persons exercise their right, a corpse that has not been buried may be donated for teaching and scientific purposes to a medical university or another university conducting teaching and research in the area of medical sciences or to a federation of entities of the system of higher education and science conducting research in the area of medical sciences. It is rightly considered that the right to question this procedure by the next of kin who have not exercised their right to burial is unjustified (Księżak, Robaczyński 2015). Donating the body of the deceased may also be a reason for not giving the body up for burial. This act should be considered a restriction of the personal rights of the relatives of the deceased. However, this does not change the fact that this act is legally binding and has all legal effects. These effects include the obligation to transfer the corpse for research (Krekora-Zając 2017).

In a situation where the corpse would neither be buried nor transferred to the medical entities mentioned above, the obligation to bury the corpse rests with the municipality having jurisdiction over the place of death.

For persons deprived of their liberty who died in prisons or detention centers, the obligation of burial rests with the prison or detention. It should be emphasized that permission for the burial of the body of a person who died in a prison is given by the public prosecutor conducting or supervising the proceedings whose object is to clarify the circumstances of the death of a person deprived of liberty or by the public prosecutor conducting or supervising preliminary actions. The detailed rules of procedure in this respect are laid down in an ordinance of the Minister of Justice (Ordinance of the MS of 7 July 2010). The content of this act includes the notification of relatives of the death, the manner of such notification, the indication of entities issuing consent for the burial of the body, the procedure for dealing with bodies that will not be collected, and the manner of bearing the costs of burial ordered by the penal institution and detention center, guided by the necessity of preserving the dignity due to the deceased and sanitary safety. In accordance with the content of the regulation, lack of willingness or ability to perform burial by entitled persons, the competent head of the county shall be informed about the possibility of transferring the remains to a public medical university or a public university conducting teaching and research activities in the area of medical sciences for scientific purposes.

Separate rules – especially in the context of notifying relatives and the procedure for dealing with a corpse that will not be collected, as well as the manner of bearing the costs of a burial ordered by a guarded center or a detention center for foreigners – apply to the procedure for dealing with the corpse of foreigners placed in a guarded center or detention center for foreigners.

Burial Space Regulations

The regulations in force do not allow for the location of burial places (graves) outside operating cemeteries. In particular, it is not permitted to carry out burials on private property (Judgment of the NSA – Intersectoral Centre in Katowice of 19 May 1997). The source of the right to a grave is a civil law contract concluded with the cemetery management by the person entitled to bury the deceased. It contains several important provisions, in particular: determination of the place of burial, type of grave and its purpose, as well as the fee and the fate of the gravestone in the event of liquidation of the cemetery or expiry of the right to the grave (Rudnicki 1999). In the opinion of the SN, the right to a grave is of two types: property and personal. The priority and decisive role are attributed to the personal elements, regardless of the value of the property elements. However, such dominance can only be spoken of when the corpse of a specific person has already been buried in a grave and the right to veneration of his or her memory has been activated (Judgment of SN of 13 February 1979). Property elements may be relevant in the absence of burial, for example, the permissibility of inheriting the right to a grave (Resolution of the SN – Civil Chamber of 2 December 1994; Judgments of the SN: of 13 February 1979, and of the panel of seven judges of 11 December 1990).

Limitations on Type and Size of Memorial

Headstones may be erected on graves that have been located following the size requirements set out above, or earth may be piled in the form of a mound over the grave. The regulations do not make restrictions on the appearance of a headstone. This is a matter of agreement between the cemetery manager and the gravestone erector. Detailed regulations in this respect may be contained in acts of local law, such as resolutions defining cemetery regulations.

Burial sites in cemeteries are divided into five possible categories. The first of these are earth graves. These graves are defined as pits in the ground into which a coffin with a corpse or urn is placed and backfilled with earth. The right to use such a grave extends for 20 years from the last burial date. The law allows for the possibility of changing an earth grave to a masonry grave, but this is rare in practice. Minimum sizes are also provided for earth graves. In the case of graves in which a child under six years of age is buried, the minimum size of the grave includes a length of 1.2 meters, a width of 0.6 meters, and a depth of 1.2 meters. Where a coffin containing the remains of an adult or a child over six years of age is buried, the minimum size of a single grave is set at 2.0 meters long, 1.0 meters wide, and 1.7 meters deep. The burial of a single urn with ashes requires a length of 0.5 meters, a width of 0.5 meters, and a depth of 0.7 meters.

The second type is masonry graves. These must also meet the required minimum dimensions of 2.2 meters in length, 0.8 meters in width, and 0.8 meters in depth for a single grave, and 0.5 meters by 0.5 meters for a single urn grave, with a minimum depth of 0.7 meters. Graves holding multiple urns should not exceed the dimensions of a single masonry grave. If coffins are placed in masonry graves, there should be a vault over each coffin and a foundation over the last coffin as insulation at least 0.3 meters thick from the vault to ground level.

The third type is family graves, which can have larger dimensions. Earthen ones should be 2.0 meters long and 1.8 meters wide regardless of depth, and masonry ones should be 2.2 meters long, 0.8 meters wide, and

0.8 meters deep. The chambers shall be separated from each other by masonry or reinforced concrete. Earthen or masonry mass graves are permitted. Earthen ones should be 2.0 meters in length and masonry ones 2.2 meters in length, and the width should be a multiple of the widths specified for family graves.

The fourth and fifth types are columbaria and catacombs. The niche in columbaria should have a uniform depth, width, and height set at a minimum of 0.4 meters. The niche in catacombs should be at least 2.0 meters by 1.0 meters horizontally, and no less than 0.9 meters high. Each is required to be separated from its neighbor by a wall at least 0.06 meters thick.

Sea burial applies to persons who have died on ships. It shall be carried out in accordance with maritime customs (Decision No.242/ MON of the Minister of Defence of 21 June 2011). If it is possible for the ship to reach the port within 24 hours, the corpse will be transported to land and buried there.

Cemeteries and Burials of the Deceased Act, 1959

Although there is no statutory definition of a cemetery, the legislator has specified that it is an area provided for in local spatial development plans for the burial of the dead (Article 3 of the Act of 31 January 1959).

A cemetery is considered open as long as it is possible to carry out burials there, i.e., as long as there are new burial places or those that can be reused. When no more burial places are available in a cemetery, a decision is taken by the competent council of the municipality (city) of the cemetery location. The decision to close religious cemeteries is taken by the competent ecclesiastical or denominational authority. In both cases, the opinion of the competent state sanitary inspector is required. Once a cemetery has been closed, it is possible to use its area for another purpose. This may occur after the lapse of 40 years from the date of the last burial of a corpse in the cemetery.

The decision to use the cemetery land for another purpose is taken by the mayor or president of the city. This purpose must follow the zoning plan. In the case of religious cemeteries, the use of land for another purpose also requires the consent of the competent authority of the church or religious association (the competent minister may dispense with the obligation to obtain consent). These authorities shall also give their opinion on how the cemetery land will be marked and commemorated. If there are monuments in the cemetery area, it is required that they be preserved, or they may be moved to another place after obtaining the consent of the provincial conservator of monuments. If a change of land use is made, the remains must be moved to another cemetery at the expense of the purchaser of the land or its new user.

Determining Which Areas in Terms of Sanitation Are Suitable for Cemeteries Regulation, 1959

The legislator has stipulated several requirements that cemeteries must meet (Article 5 Act of 31 January 1959). They must be located within a fenced area, which must be sanitary, and must have a pre-burial house or a mortuary which will be used to store the bodies of deceased persons until they are buried, to examine human remains for forensic, sanitary, or police purposes, and to perform other activities related to the burial of remains. Detailed regulations on what sanitary requirements a funeral home or mortuary should meet and how to store a corpse or remains are contained in the implementing regulation (Ordinance of the MZ of 23 March 2011). Separate legal solutions apply to the handling of corpses and remains (Ordinance of the MZ of 7 December 2001). The ordinance indicates how to deal with corpses after a person's death and contains solutions dedicated to the death of persons who died due to a SARS-CoV-2 infection.

Establishment, Enlargement, and Design of Cemeteries

The possibility of establishing and expanding cemeteries is the task of the municipal authorities and the authorities of churches and religious associations (the Law on Cemeteries, Starzecka 2014). The establishment or expansion of a municipal cemetery is decided by the municipal council and, in cities with district rights, by the city council, while the relevant church authorities decide on the establishment or expansion of a religious cemetery. An analogy applies to decisions to close a cemetery. Such decisions must be subject to the opinion of the state sanitary inspector.

Cemeteries should be maintained as green areas with a park-like layout, where the existing greenery is subject to protection against destruction (Ordinance of the Minister of ME of 25 August 1959; Sobczak 2003). Management of municipal cemeteries – it is assumed that management means the performance of cemetery services for the benefit of cemetery users (Kalisz, Kowalczyk 2011) – is the responsibility of the competent mayors, depending on the location of the cemetery, while management of religious cemeteries[2] is the responsibility of religious associations. The management of a cemetery is also within the competence of churches, although this is not directly apparent from the law's wording. However, given the fact that the legislator used the term "competent ecclesiastical authorities" concerning their competence to establish cemeteries, it should be concluded that the competence of religious associations and churches is understood in the same way (Starzecka 2014).

The competence of cemetery managers is broad and includes deciding on the establishment (in the case of a municipal cemetery, this decision is made by the municipal council in the form of a resolution), expansion, and closure of the cemetery. These entities also decide the size and area of the cemetery, as well as the rules of accepting the remains for burial, collecting fees, keeping records, supervising safety, rules of conducting funerals, and issuing regulations concerning the rights and obligations of entities using the cemetery. It should be emphasized that establishing religious cemeteries does not constitute a religious or ecclesiastical investment, but it is a public-purpose investment (Rudnicki 1999). Decisions taken by the founders and managers of a cemetery must comply with the requirements of spatial planning and sanitary guidelines. Establishing a cemetery first requires preparing a zoning plan and then a resolution to establish a cemetery by the competent municipal authority (Hrynicki 2013).

The appropriate legal solutions exclude the possibility of establishing a cemetery in an area other than that which is included in the spatial development plans. Cemeteries may also not be established by natural persons and legal entities under private law (Rudnicki 1999). On the other hand, churches and religious associations have a full right to build, expand and maintain religious facilities as long as they comply with the requirements of Polish law (see Chapter 10. 3: Religious cemeteries).

The optimal site for a cemetery, according to the applicable law, in terms of location, must meet the criteria listed in the abovementioned Requirements (2008).

According to the current Polish regulations and practice, the area needed to establish a cemetery is calculated in compliance with the formula:

$$a \times 23 \times 4, 5m^2 = p,$$

where

a – average annual number of deaths in a given locality
23 – the rate resulting from the reuse of a grave for burial before the expiration of 20 years and the presumed number of incidents of extension for a further period
4,5 m^2 – burial site
p – burial area – these are the places designated for earthen and masonry graves, as well as for the interment of corpses and remains in catacombs and columbaria.

The "p" value should account for about 40%–60% of the total area of the cemetery. The rest of the area should be used for greenery, roads, squares, utility and administrative buildings, and a pre-burial house (mortuary) (Drembkowski 2018).

The process of establishing a cemetery includes:

- Site selection for the cemetery. Since the cemetery may pose a significant threat to the environment, including groundwater, hence the decision of the State District Sanitary Inspectorate to have jurisdiction over the project site is necessary. The sanitary service verifies whether the site meets the aforementioned conditions in terms of location, and natural and geological characteristics on the basis of complete, up-to-date geotechnical documentation taking into account the properties of the land, water relations, depth, variability of the groundwater level, and existing plant communities.
- Adoption of a spatial development plan for the area predestined for a cemetery. Preparation of the forecast is the fulfillment of a legal obligation under the Act of 3 October 2008. The purpose of the forecast is to determine the nature of probable impacts on the natural environment, which may be caused by the implementation of development and land-use methods prescribed or permitted by the plan.
- It is necessary to obtain permission to change the predestination of agricultural land for non-agricultural and non-forest purposes if the planned cemetery is to be located on land subject to protection. The NSA specifies that the change of land use in a spatial development plan for non-agricultural and non-forest purposes should be preceded by a request for consent, citing the provisions of the Act of 3 February 1995.
- Adoption of a resolution of the municipal council on the establishment of a municipal cemetery. The resolution should include the date of establishment and indicate the location and area of the newly established site for the cemetery.
- Obtaining construction permit. The basis for the issuance of a building permit is the construction design for the cemetery. This project should include, as required, the results of geological-engineering studies and geotechnical conditions for the foundation of buildings.
- Construction of cemetery.
- Use of cemetery. The maintenance and management of a cemetery is the responsibility of its owners, i.e., the religious or municipal authorities. A cemetery shall be maintained as a green area with a park-like layout. Use of the facility shall be conducted in accordance with the cemetery's site plan.

At the same time, there are legal acts that classify a cemetery as a green area. In the Act of 16 April 2004, a cemetery is classified as a green area which is defined as areas decorated together with technical infrastructure and buildings functionally associated with them, covered with vegetation, performing public functions, and in particular parks, greenery, promenades, boulevards, botanical gardens, zoos, cemeteries, greenery accompanying the roads on the grounds of the buildings, squares, historic fortifications, buildings, landfills, airports, railway stations and industrial facilities. Additionally, in the Act of 27 March 2003, the term "greenery of cemeteries" is used for a necropolis. Moreover, the Ordinance of 7 March 2008 obliges managers to establish and maintain cemeteries as park sites.

The responsibility for the quality of construction facilities, including cemeteries, rests with those who perform an independent technical function in construction (i.e., who have a building license) (Giedych, Szumański 2008). The design of a cemetery is prepared on a basic map for design purposes, based on the dispositions in the adopted spatial development plan.

Cemetery projects are developed in a bidding procedure (announcement of public procurement) or a competition procedure (announcement of a design competition).

The development of the designed cemetery should include:

- A permanent fence, with a minimum height of 1.5 meters
- A burial area constituting 40%–60% of the total area allocated for the cemetery site.
- Isolating and decorative greenery, in particular, lawns, shrubs, and trees.
- Roads, walking, and pedestrian routes.
- Parking spaces (if not provided outside the cemetery site).
- Toilets (if not provided outside the cemetery site).
- Waste collection areas.
- Water points.
- Land necessary for a funeral home, with size and functionality adapted to local needs.

In addition, in cases justified by local needs, a chapel, administrative and economic facilities should also be included.

Passages between the graves should have a width of no less than 50 centimeters.

When designing a burial area, it should be allocated:

- About 60% of the area for ordinary graves without masonry rights, including 15% for graves of children under six years of age.
- About 10% for individual rows of earth or masonry graves.

- About 20% for family graves.
- About 1%–5% for fields or Alley of Honour.
- About 5% for fields for urns.

According to articles 1 and 3 of the Act of 31 January 1959, the expansion of a cemetery may take place in a site allocated for this purpose in the spatial development plan after obtaining the consent of the right sanitary inspector. Filling up the available burial space and the inability to meet the legal requirements for the construction of a new cemetery implies the need to expand the existing facilities, very often with historic status. Any works undertaken on the historic site require agreement with the locally competent provincial monument conservator (Pasierb 1995; Rudkowski 2003).

The extension of a cemetery involves earthworks (including landscaping), roadworks (construction of roads, terrain stairs, utility yards, protection of slopes against landslides and soil erosion), construction of technical infrastructure (rainwater drainage, water supply system, lighting), installation of small architecture elements (benches, fencing, water points), and greenery works (making lawns, planting trees and shrubs, and maintaining them). The expansion of a cemetery takes into account the purchase of land, felling of trees (including clearing and planting), over-surfacing of the area to enable burials, fencing of the area, hardening of driveways, construction of passages from the existing cemetery to the area of its extension, and elements of internal communication, development of the area (water supply, electricity), possible realization of cubic elements (pre-burial house, chapel, mortuary) while maintaining, emphasizing the assets of the historic part of the cemetery.

The following regularities emerge from the legal regulations and Polish practice of cemetery development:

- Communication accessibility. The development of a cemetery extension is carried out with reference to the existing, used facility, with particular attention paid to ensuring internal communication and spatial links.
- Securing the area for cemetery services (small commerce and administration), allowing for the opening of a pre-burial house, chapel, mortuary, and technical and economic service facilities (particularly important if there were no such facilities in the cemetery area before the extension).
- Respect for natural assets. Ensuring in the process of the cemetery expansion the continuity of plant and animal species, together with the habitats of ecosystems, making a detailed inventory of the greenery before starting any expansion works, and minimal interference with

the tree stand, necessary for the realization of the planned functions, leaving the oldest and most valuable specimens.

Notes

1 From the 1st of January 2023, the death card will consist of three parts intended, respectively, for the registration of death; for the cemetery administration, and for public statistics. Its model will be determined by the minister in charge of health, in agreement with the minister in charge of internal affairs and the minister in charge of information technology (replacement: *Journal of Laws* of 2014, item 1741 and 1888, of 2015, item 2281 and of 2017, item 1524).
2 A municipal cemetery is a cemetery owned by a municipality or inter-municipal association, and a denominational cemetery is a cemetery owned or held in perpetual usufruct by a church or another religious association or legal entity.

References

Act of 15 May 2015 amending the Law on cemeteries and burying the dead, the Law on graves and war cemeteries, and the Law on the Institute of National Remembrance – Commission for the Prosecution of Crimes against the Polish Nation (JoL 2015, item. 935).
Act of 16 April 2004 on Nature Protection (JoL 2022 item. 916)
Act of 23 April 1964 Civil Code (JoL 1964 No.16 item. 93).
Act of 27 March 2003 on Spatial Planning and Development (JoL 2022 item. 503).
Act of 28 March 1933 on war graves and cemeteries (JoL 2018 item. 2337).
Act of 28 November 2014 on civil status records (JoL 2014 item. 1741).
Act of 3 October 2008 on the provision of information on the environment and its protection, public participation in environmental protection and environmental impact assessments (JoL 2022 item. 1029).
Act of 31 January 1959 on cemeteries and burial of the deceased (ct. JoL 2020, item. 1947).
Act of 4 July 1991 on the Relationship of the State to the Polish Autocephalous Orthodox Church (JoL 2014 item. 1726).
Act of 6 June 1997 Criminal Code (JoL 1997 No.88 item. 553).
Act of 7 July 1994 Building Law [UPB] (JoL 2021 item. 2351).
Burial rules for the Navy are set out in Decision No.242/MON of the Minister of Defence of 21 June 2011 on the implementation of the Rules of Service on Navy Ships.
Case of Solska and Rybicka v. Poland, application nos. 30491/17 and 31083/17, ECtHR judgment of 20 September 2018.
Długozima Anna 2020, "Lokalizacja współczesnych cmentarzy komunalnych w Polsce" (Location of contemporary communal cemeteries in Poland), *Prace Geograficzne*, No. 161, 81–106.
Długozima Anna 2020, "Social infrastructure of burial nature in Poland by voivodeships – conditions and changes", *Acta Sci. Pol., Administratio Locorum* 19(1), 19–31.

Draft of 21 November 2019 Act of................ .... on ascertaining, documenting and registering deaths, https://legislacja.rcl.gov.pl/docs//2/12327506/12643140/12643141/dokument428071.pdf.

Drembkowski Paweł 2018, *Ustawa o cmentarzach i chowaniu zmarłych. Komentarz* (Cemeteries and Burials of the Deceased Act. Commentary), C.H. Beck, Warszawa.

Giedych Renata, Szumański Marek 2008, *Krajobraz z paragrafem. Architekt krajobrazu – wybrane aspekty prawne wykonywania zawodu* (Landscape with a Paragraph. Landscape architect – selected legal aspects of practising the profession), SGGW, Warszawa

Hrynicki Wojciech. M 2013, "Zakładanie, rozszerzanie i utrzymywanie cmentarzy – przyczynek do dyskusji" (Establishment, expansion, and maintenance of cemeteries – contributing to the discussion), *Administracja: Teoria, Dydaktyka, Praktyka* 4(33).

Judgment of SN of 13 February 1979I CR 25/79.

Judgment of SN of 31 March 1980, II CR 88/80.

Judgment of the NSA of 5 October 2021. II GSK 1275/21, LEX nr 3266973.

Judgment of the SN of 11 November 1976, II CR 415/76.

Judgment of the SN of 13 January 1965, I CR 646/64.

Judgment of the SN of 16 June 1998, I CKN 729/97.

Judgment of the SN of 17 February 2016, III CSK 84/15.

Judgment of the SN of 19 November 2020, II CSK 30/19, LEX nr 3082395.

Judgment of the SN of 23 May 1975, II CR 193/75.

Judgment of the SN of 25 September 1972, II CR 353/72.

Judgment of the SN of 29 January 2003, I CKN 1453/00.

Judgment of the SN of 6 February 2008, II CSK 474/07

Judgment of the SN of 6 November 1978, IV CR 359/78.

Judgment of the SN of 7 June 1966, I CR 346/65.

Judgments of the SN: of 13 February 1979, I CR 25/79 and of the panel of seven judges of 11 December 1990, III CRN 455/90 – unpublished.

Judgment of the Supreme Administrative Court in Katowice of 19 May1997, SA/Ka 1717/95, (in:) 'Wokanda' 1998, no. 2.

Kalisz Anna, Kowalczyk Ewa 2011, "Świadczenie usług cmentarnych i pogrzebowych a uprawnienia zarządcy cmentarza w świetle ustawy antymonopolowej. Studium przypadku Kościoła Rektoralnego w Lublinie" (Provision of cemetery and funeral services, and the powers of the cemetery administrator under the Antimonopoly Act. A case study of the Rectoral Church in Lublin), *Radca Prawny*, 2011, No. 2.

Krekora-Zając Dorota 2017, "Akt donacji zwłok ludzkich (uwagi de lege lata i de lege ferenda)", (The act of donating a human corpse (de lege lata and de lege ferenda remarks)), *Państwo i Prawo*, No. 11.

Księżak Paweł, Robaczyński Wojciech 2012, "Skuteczność woli zmarłego co do jego pochówku i sprawowania kultu jego pamięci" (Effectiveness of the will of the deceased as to his burial and the exercise of the cult of his memory), *Palestra*, No. 9-10.

Księżak Paweł, Robaczyński Wojciech 2015, "Dysponowanie zwłokami ludzkimi dla celów naukowych i medycznych" (Disposing of human remains for scientific and medical purposes), *Państwo i Prawo*, No. 1.

Niewiadomski Zbigniew 2003, *Planowanie przestrzenne. Zarys systemu* (Spatial planning. Legal framework), Wydawnictwo Prawnicze LexisNexis, Warszawa.

Nowicki Marek Antoni 2019, *Ekshumacja ofiar katastrofy smoleńskiej.* (Exhumation of Victims of the 2010 Smolensk Catastrophe. Discussion of the ECtHR judgment of 20 September 2018,30491/17 Solska and Rybicka), LEX/el.

Ordinance of 7 March 2008 of the Minister of Infrastructure on requirements on requirements for 513 cemeteries, graves and other places of burial of corpses and remains (JoL 2008, No. 48, item. 284).

Ordinance of the MS of 7 July 2010 on the manner of handling the bodies of persons deprived of liberty who died in penal institutions and detention centres (JoL 2010 No. 123, item. 839).

Ordinance of the MZ of 23 March 2011 on the manner of storage of bodies and remains (JoL 2011 No. 75, item. 405).

Ordinance of the MZ of 27 December 2007 on the issue of permits and certificates for the transport of human remains and cadavers (JoL 2007 No. 249 item. 1866).

Ordinance of the MZ of 7 December 2001 on the handling of remains and human remains (consolidated text JoL 2021, item. 1910).

Ordinance of the MZiOS of 3 August 1961 on the declaration of death and its cause (JoL 1961 No. 39, item. 202).

Ordinance of the Minister of Municipal Economy of 25 August 1959 on determining which areas are suitable for cemeteries from the sanitary point of view (Journal of Laws, No. 52, item 315).

Pasierb Jan Stanisław 1995, *Ochrona zabytków sztuki kościelnej* (Protection of ecclesiastical art monuments), Biblioteka Towarzystwa Opieki nad Zabytkami, Warszawa.

PKOB 1999, *Polska Klasyfikacja Obiektów Budowlanych* (Polish Classification of Building Facilities). http://prawo.sejm.gov.pl/isap.nsf/download.xsp/ [12.02.2022].

Resolution of the SN – Civil Chamber of 2 December 1994, III CZP 155/94, OSP 1995/6, item. 134 and OSNC 1995/3, item. 52.

Rudkowski Tadeusz Maria 2003, "O ochronę cmentarzy zabytkowych" (For the protection of historical cemeteries), *Ochrona Zabytków*, No. 1/2, 104–114.

Rudnicki Stanisław 1999, *Prawo do Grobu. Zagadnienia Cywilistyczne* (Right to the Grave. Civil Law Issues), Zakamycze, Kraków.

Sierpowska Iwona 2020, *Rejestracja zgonu i postępowanie ze zwłokami* [in:] Śmierć w ujęciu prawa administracyjnego, (Registration of Death and handling of corpses) [in:] Death in terms of administrative law, Warsaw.

Sobczak Aleksander 2003, *Poradnik cmentarny. Kościelne i cywilne normy prawne o cmentarzach i chowaniu zmarłych, wraz z orzecznictwem* (Cemetery Handbook. Ecclesiastical and civil legal norms on cemeteries and the burial of the deceased, including case law), Gaudentinum, Gniezno.

Starzecka Katarzyna 2014, "Lokalizacja cmentarza wyznaniowego w świetle przepisów prawa polskiego o planowaniu i zagospodarowaniu przestrzennym" (Location of a religious cemetery in the light of the Polish law on planning and spatial development), *St.zPr.Wyz*, no. 17.

Wedeł-Domaradzka Agnieszka 2021, *Prawo do pochówku i prawo do sprawowania kultu w odniesieniu do osób zasłużonych wobec państwa i społeczeństwa - de lege lata i de lege ferenda* (The right to burial and the right to worship concerning persons of merit to the state and society - de lege lata and de lege ferenda), [in:] *Prawa zmarłych?* (Rights of the dead?), ed. Krzysztof Motyka, Lublin Publishing House of the Catholic University of Lublin.

5 Governance

Anna Długozima and
Agnieszka Wedeł-Domaradzka

Local Government Structure

Poland has a three-tier structure in local government (self-government). The lowest level of organization is the municipality. As the lowest-level units and the ones that are closest to the citizens, communes are involved in solving the problems of their inhabitants (Act of 28 March 1933 on war graves and cemeteries). The commune council is the decision-making body, and the mayor or president is the executive body. The executive body's name depends on the municipality's population, size, and status – rural, rural-urban, or urban.

At a higher level are the counties. The county council is the decision-making body, while its executive body is the county management board, headed by the starost. The tasks of the district are defined in a similar way to those of the municipality. However, they are carried out on a supra-municipal level, i.e., to the extent that their implementation in smaller units would be organizationally or economically unjustified.

On the highest level in the local government structure are the voivodeships. The tasks of the voivodeships focus on policy planning and activities of a strategic nature. The provincial assembly carries these out as the decision-making body, whereas the provincial board acts as the executive body. The voivodeship is the only structure in which a government administration body, the voivode, functions alongside the self-governing body. In addition, the provincial governor performs tasks related to managing war cemeteries (Article 5a, Act of 28 March 1933 on war graves and cemeteries).

From the perspective of burials and cemeteries, the most important is the municipality. It is the municipalities, as already indicated, that decide on the location of cemeteries in the relevant resolution of the municipal council. The municipal authorities are also obliged to carry out burials if no one undertakes this task. This obligation results from the Act of 12 March 2004 on social assistance; following it is an obligatory task for

DOI: 10.4324/9781003207634-5

the municipality. The manner of providing a funeral is determined by the municipality, most often in a resolution of the municipal council. Tasks related to cemeteries, burial grounds, and memorials are reserved for the municipalities.

Public Enterprises

The municipality can be an economic participant, have property, and manage this property independently (Niewiadomski 2003). There is no central entity responsible for burials in Poland. The municipality's obligatory tasks include establishing and maintaining cemeteries. Municipalities are also obliged to provide proper sanitary and technical conditions for cemeteries as well as finance their maintenance (Lis, 2019). The receipts from charges for cemetery services constitute the municipality's own income. Maintaining and administering municipal cemeteries belongs to municipality heads, town mayors, and city mayors. In practice, these tasks are frequently delegated to municipality-owned enterprises and local government budgetary establishments, and less frequently to contractors chosen by means of public procurement. However, delegating most tasks to external entities does not exempt the municipality officials from the obligation to control and supervise (NIK 2016, Lis 2019). In order to perform public tasks jointly, it is permissible to establish an inter-municipal association for cemeteries. A resolution to establish such an association is adopted by the councils of relevant municipalities (Niewiadomski 2003).

Private Companies

Under current legislation, it is not possible way for private operators to enter the cemetery market to establish private cemeteries. Despite the ban on private operators, the NIK report (2016) shows that as many as 37% of the communes surveyed had their cemetery fees set by external operators, driven by economic calculation. Local government bodies have the right to delegate the management and administration of a cemetery to a contractor selected through a public procurement procedure (NIK 2016). A municipality that has outsourced the management of a cemetery should regularly check that the tasks entrusted to the contractor are carried out correctly. The company selected on the basis of a request for proposal is responsible for the direct execution of the burial. These companies usually provide a comprehensive service, from dealing with the body of the deceased to carrying out the burial and providing the necessary burial elements (coffin, urn). They also take care of the body's transport and ensure that the burial site is properly marked.

Public-Private Partnerships (PPP)

PPP is understood as a partnership of the public and the private sector, aimed at realizing enterprises and rendering services commonly provided by the public sector.

The legal frame of PPP, existing in Polish law since 2009, enables private entrepreneurs to build cemeteries with ceremonial facilities on land made available by district councils at their own expense to further exploit them for several dozen years, which scheme is aimed at disburdening tight district budgets. The construction of cemeteries and cemetery infrastructure is carried out under a PPP in the form of concession (Deloitte 2014). The flagship cemetery projects implemented in Poland in the PPP idea are the construction of a municipal cemetery in Podgórki Tynieckie (Kraków) and a complex of columbaria in the city of Gdańsk.

Professional Funeral Organizations

Two separate national organizations – the Polish Funeral Association (PSP) and the Polish Funeral Chamber (PIP) – endeavor to control the numerically dispersed market of funeral parlors, casket and funeral supplies manufacturers and cemetery and crematory administrators.

PSP is the largest and oldest funeral association in Poland. It was based in Warsaw, and commenced its operation throughout Poland in 1998. The main objects of the Association as per its Articles are: cooperating with central government bodies, local authorities, undertakers, clergymen, insurance agents, and cemetery equipment and funeral supplies manufacturers; giving opinions on bills and orders to relevant ministries; preparing expert evaluations concerning the situation on the funeral, crematory, and cemetery services market for local authorities; improving qualifications by organizing trade conferences and workshops. PSP has been a national member of FIAT-IFTA since 2006. Since 2021, the position of FIAT-IFTA president has been held by Marek Cichewicz (the first Pole elected to this top position). PSP, together with the MTP Group, was the patron of the Wojciech Krawczyk MEMENTO Funeral Fair from 2012 to 2022. On 4 March 2022, an agreement was signed under which it was decided that the fair would not be organized in its current format. As a result of the Deregulation Act coming into force and the abolition of the Licensed Property Manager qualification as of 31 December 2013, the Association, upholding professionalism and the possession of specialist knowledge and skills in the management of cemetery properties, has introduced a Central Register of Cemetery Estate Managers called the 'Professional ID Card'.

PIP was set up in 2002, embracing small and average-sized companies operating in the broadly defined funeral sector. Their activities include legal and accounting consultancy; furthering the trade interests in relations with central government bodies and local authorities and, where justified, before courts of general jurisdiction; co-participating in the legislative process by appearing and giving opinions on amendments to the laws applicable to the funeral trade; in-service training for member companies and their personnel. The NECROEXPO in Kielce is an event organized in partnership with the Polish Funeral Chamber.

Four titles lead the Polish funeral press market: the bimonthly *Memento*, the monthly *Funeral Culture* , the quarterly *Bulletin of the Polish Funeral Chamber*, and the quarterly *OMEGA*. The Journals are devoted to funeral culture and organization, activities of cemeteries and funeral parlors, funeral law, as well as funeral and cemetery service technology. Memento, with a maximum circulation of 1,000, is a subscription journal published by the PSP. It is the oldest funeral journal in Poland, founded in 1997. The*Bulletin of the Polish Funeral Chamber* is a free quarterly for members. *Funeral Culture* has been published since 2004. Since 2015, the MTP Group has published the magazine *OMEGA – Idea Book for the Funeral Industry*. This quarterly magazine is distributed free of charge to 2,422 funeral homes, crematoriums, and cemetery managers throughout Poland.

References

Act of 12 March 2004 on social assistance (JoL of 2021, item. 2268).

Act of 28 March 1933 on war graves and cemeteries (JoL of 2018, item. 2337).

Deloitte 2014, *Polish Construction Companies 2013 – key players, development and diversification prospects.* https://www2.deloitte.com/ [12.04.2022].

Lis Piotr 2019, "Negotiations, expropriation and compensation for establishing cemeteries in Poland an overview of the subject matter", *Acta Universitatis Lodziensis Folia Geographica Socio-Oeconomica*, 35, 47–57.

Niewiadomski Zbigniew 2003, *Planowanie przestrzenne. Zarys systemu* (Spatial planning. Legal framework), LexisNexis, Warszawa.

NIK 2016, *Zarządzanie cmentarzami komunalnymi* (Municipal cemeteries management). https://www.nik.gov.pl/plik/id,12230,vp,14613.pdf [12.04.2022].

6   Religious Beliefs and Funerary Practices of the Churches

Anna E. Kubiak and Anna Długozima

The Catholic Church

The Catholic faith emphasizes the role of purgatory as the initial stage on the way to heaven and the danger of being condemned to hell. The main idea in the liturgy of a funeral is the emphasis on the paschal character of the Christian's death. The chosen prayers, psalms, and sermons are to express hope for resurrection and eternal life. Hence, the Mass for the Dead is called the "Mass of the Resurrection" (Kramer 2007, 227). The church introduced its religious practices: sprinkling, anointing, and prayer. The rosary became the most popular prayer for the relief of the soul.

The rite of the liturgy of the Catholic Church during a funeral consists of three stations, although, depending on local customs and conditions, they are limited to the last two (in the city) or only the last one (e.g., sometimes at cremations). The first station takes place at home. An invited priest sprinkles the body with holy water and says a prayer. The second station takes place in the church. The coffin is placed on the catafalque, with its feet at the altar. Candles are lit, and a candle is lit at the headstone. A Mass is said for the intention of the deceased. After the Mass, the priest sprinkles the coffin with holy water three times and then incenses it three times. Exhortation, accompanying the procession to the grave, is an important part of the second station. A bell is rung at the entrance to the cemetery. The third station takes place at the grave and consists of the prayers of the priest and those gathered. After the sprinkling of the coffin, which used to be accompanied by throwing a lump of earth on it along with the words, "From dust you were made and to dust you shall return", it is lowered down into the grave.

In Poland, the participation of priests and church liturgy is incomparably greater than in Europe. Although the funeral home is the main director of the rite, the roles of lay and church officiants are constantly negotiated. Many priests are against the intermediation of contacts with the family of the deceased. They expect to meet with

DOI: 10.4324/9781003207634-6

the deceased's closest relatives and want to have more influence on the funeral scenario, such as the date of the Mass and the time of burial. The religious practice of the deceased parishioner can be problematic. Pastors collect data on a parishioner's practice and may refuse a church funeral, but this – sometimes overcome via an additional fee – rarely happens. Many funeral directors lament the problem of a 'thanks offering' for the celebration of a funeral liturgy. In Poland around 90% of funerals follow the Catholic ceremony and around 10% are secular (the exact data are not accessible, as no institution gathers such information) or are carried out in line with other religious faiths (Kubiak 2015).

The Orthodox Church

According to the current GUS report (2022), Orthodox Christianity, the Polish Autocephalous Orthodox Church ("Polski Autokefaliczny Kościół Prawosławny" in Polish), with about 504,000 members, is Poland's second-largest religion. The number of all Orthodox believers in Poland is estimated to be 1.3% of the population. The number of Orthodox faithful in Poland has grown in recent years. One reason for this increase has been the unprecedented influx of Ukrainian immigrants. The tradition of Eastern Christianity in Poland has its beginning nearly in the 9th century, the times of brothers Cyril and Methodius's saint missions. It gained complete independence (autocephaly) in 1925. Today, Polish Orthodoxy is very diverse, influenced by the change of borders after WWII and the migration of the population to the East, as well as the "Vistula" action, resulting in the overwhelming number of Orthodox Christians from the South and Middle East of Polish lands being deported in 1947 (Romanowicz 2015). The Eastern Orthodox Church in Poland is divided into six dioceses.

According to Orthodox theology, a man after death is still keeping his awareness (Fiedorczuk et al. 2013). Until a funeral takes place, the deceased's body should be shown openly in church, a family home, or a funeral parlor. According to the Orthodox tradition, the layman's body is washed before the funeral and dressed in new secular clothes – as a sign of adopting immortality (Fiedorczuk et al. 2013). A funeral liturgy is exercised on the third day after death. In the time before the funeral, the family and relatives should pray for the deceased's spirit. The funeral liturgy is called *Panichida*.

After the funeral ceremony, it is necessary to set a date for divine services with a priest. In the Orthodox tradition, these services are done on the ninth and fortieth day after death and on the anniversary. The Orthodox Church strictly forbids the body's cremation. Orthodox believers visit the graves of their relatives on the ninth day after Easter, during a feast called *Radunica*. At this time, Masses are celebrated for the dead. Flowers and Easter eggs are placed on graves, usually in red as a sign of Christ's shed blood and His resurrection (Olej-Kobus et al. 2009).

The Protestant Churches

The community of Protestants consists of around 120,000 believers (GUS 2022). In total, there are about 100 denominations belonging to various streams of Protestantism, which makes Protestants the most numerous in terms of the number of registered churches and other religious associations with regulated legal status (Pasek 2020). The fourth largest religion in Poland is the Lutherans – members of the Evangelical Church of the Augsburg Confession (60,425 believers) – who constitute 0.18% of the whole population (GUS 2022). Moreover, The Evangelical Church of the Augsburg Confession is the oldest among the Protestant Churches in Poland. Today there are six dioceses of this Church in Poland: Cieszyńska (with 35,388 believers), Katowicka (12,711), Mazurska (3,300), Pomorsko-Wielkopolska (2,428), Warszawska (4,066) and Wrocławska (2,532) (GUS 2019). Thus, in its territorial and administrative structure, this Church refers significantly to the spatial concentration of the original clusters of Lutheran adherents. They are concentrated mainly in north-eastern Poland and in the south.

The history of the Evangelical Church of the Augsburg Confession in Poland begins with the Reformation movement (Kowalik 2010; CEC 2019). The first Protestant believers appeared in Poland around 1518. The complete partitioning of Poland by Russia, Austria and Prussia in 1795 opened a new phase of religious history. Large Lutheran congregations were formed in the cities. Cieszyn, Gdańsk, Poznań, Toruń, Szlichtyngowa, Wschowa were the centres of the Polish Lutheran universe. In Prussia's part of Poland, strong congregations developed in Silesia. Accordingly, a large Protestant community lives in the Śląskie Voivodeship – over 70% of all members of the Evangelical Church of the Augsburg Confession (GUS 2022). Due to their turbulent past, many Protestant churches were changed into Catholic ones after WWII (Rykała 2009; Rogowska 2014). Act of 13 May 1994 on the Relationship of the State to the Evangelical-Augsburg Church in the Republic of Poland in Article 28 states that parishes have the right to own, manage, establish and expand burial cemeteries (Drembkowski 2018).

There is no cult of the dead, but the constant memory and care of graves is cultivated. It is not customary in the Lutheran tradition to light a candle 'for the soul of the dead'. If the Lutherans light candles on graves (this is not practised in all regions of Poland), it is only in remembrance, but without a prayerful intention. When visiting the graves of relatives, they bring flowers or wreaths. At the same time, it is emphasized not to buy plastic candles and artificial flowers, bearing in mind climate protection. In Lutheran tradition, the dead are re-membered on the last Sunday of the church year, the so-called Eternity Sunday (end of November). Lutherans in Poland may be buried or cremated, depending on the preferences of the person who has died and their family.

Judaism

Judaism is the oldest non-Slavic religious tradition in Poland. The first mention of the Jews in Polish territory dates back to the 10th century, and the first official Polish document granting privileges and autonomy to them was the Statute of Kalisz from the 13th century. According to statistics by Samuel Gruber and Phyllis Myers (1995), in 1939 there were 1,415 Jewish communities comprised of at least 100 people (every Jewish commune had at least one synagogue and its own cemetery). The Jewish presence in Poland was brutally interrupted by WWII, during which 3 million Jews died (Worldmark Encyclopedia of Religious Practices 2015). After 1989, there was a revival of Jewish life in Poland. A number of people returned to their Jewish roots and new organizations were established to develop the life of the Jewish community. The oldest association is the Union of Jewish Religious Communities, which rep-resents traditional, orthodox Judaism (Pasek 2020). The Union com-prises 10 communities in Warsaw, Kraków, Legnica, Łódź, Wrocław, Szczecin, Bielsko-Biała, Katowice, Poznań and Gdańsk (1,704 believers). The main task of the association is to organize the religious and cultural life of its members. The organization provides care, organizational and maintenance activities, and takes care of the existing synagogues and houses of prayer and Jewish cemeteries (GUS 2022).

Jewish communities have Chevra Kadisha – a Holy Society, whose sole function is to ensure dignified treatment of the deceased in accordance with Jewish law, custom, and tradition. According to Jewish tradition, the body of the deceased should be buried within 24 hours after death. The followers of Judaism commemorate the dead at anni-versaries of death (Yahrzeit), when they light a special candle *jorcajtowa* for 24 hours to honor the memory of the dead. The specificity of Jewish cemeteries stems from the fact that, according to its traditions and laws, human remains are sacred even after death. Therefore, Jewish cemeteries cannot be disturbed. The remains of the deceased can only be exhumed in order to be moved to a family grave, to the Holy Land, from a non-Jewish cemetery to a Jewish one, or if threatened with desecration or natural phenomena, e.g., flood. Jews do not adorn graves with flowers. They light candles on them and, in the case of the graves of religious leaders (rabbis and tzaddikim), leave pieces of paper with pleas to God written on them. Over their graves specific structures, called *ohels*, are erected. They create a separate space where pilgrims can pray, lay *kwitlech*, and light candles, providing those praying with protection from adverse weather conditions (Bielawski 2017). Ohels of more than 60 tzaddikim are located in 35 towns and cities. The most well-known are Leżajsk, Nowy Sącz, Lublin, Góra Kalwaria, Bobowa, and Lelów. More information about Jewish funeral rites can be found in Aleksandra Wilczura (2010) and Washington Hebrew Congregation publications.

Other Faith Groups

Jehovah's Witnesses are the third largest religious organization in Poland. According to the GUS report (2022), they have about 115,000 members in Poland. Jehovah's Witnesses were officially registered in Poland in 1989. They claim death is a punishment for Adam's disobedience to Jehovah. According to the beliefs of the Jehovah's Witnesses, death does not take the dead to a better world but puts an end to all human actions. They do not believe in spirits of the dead; therefore, they reject practices resulting from the view that a human has an immortal soul. Funeral ceremonies do not include rituals for the dead, such as, e.g., a wake, or sacrifices. The faith does not have any prohibitions against cremation. A Jehovah's Witnesses funeral service is similar to those of other Christian faiths but lasts only 15 or 30 minutes. They do not celebrate All Saints' Day, and they do not put up candles. There are no crosses at the graves of Jehovah's Witnesses. This is mainly because they consider worshiping symbols to be idolatry, which the Bible condemns (Krajewska-Kułak et al. 2013).

Islam is an old phenomenon, deeply rooted in the history and culture of Poland (Dziekan 2011). As Agata Nalborczyk and Paweł Borecki (2011, 343) stated:

> thanks to the centuries-long presence of Tatars in Poland, Islam is an officially recognized denomination and the position of Muslims is much better than that of other religious minorities.

The group, which believes in Islam and has lived in Polish territory for generations, is known as the Tatars. The Polish-Lithuanian Tatars make up the core of Polish Islam. The Tatars have created their own kind of Islam, named by Katarzyna Warmińska (1999) as 'Tatar Islam'. Apart from the syncretic character of their religion, they follow the basic rules of Islam. Tatars are descendants of Mongols, who came with the armies of Genghis Khan's descendants, as well as of local Turkic–speaking peoples. The first Tatars appeared in Polish lands in the 14th century and most of them are descendants of the Tatar population who arrived in Poland in the 17th century. Nowadays, the Tatar ethnic group, which is made up of more than five thousand members, lives mostly in the territory in the north-eastern part of Poland. Muslim communities exist in Warsaw, Białystok, Bohoniki, Kruszyniany, Gdańsk, Poznań and Bydgoszcz. Bohoniki and Kruszyniany are traditional religious locations of the Tatars' community. Tatars are also still living in Krynki and Sokółka to this day (Nalborczyk, Borecki 2011). The Muslim Association of the Capital City of Warsaw and the Muslim Religious Union in the Polish Republic were established in the interwar period with the aim to consolidate Islam believers. In order to meet the needs of the growing Muslim community in Poland, the Muslim League in the Republic of Poland (15,500 members) was registered in 2004 (GUS 2022).

The most important Muslim rite from the cycle of life is the burial ceremony. The followers of Islam believe in the resurrection of the body after death and the Last Judgment. According to religious law, a Muslim needs to be buried within three days after his death. In Poland, Muslims bury their dead in coffins, which are placed in modest graves, and always facing Mecca. Contemporary Muslim graves do not differ from Christian ones (with the exception of symbols and writings). Graves are arranged in regular rows called *sefs* and covered with field stones. The largest stone is placed at the head and the smallest at the feet of the deceased (Kołodziejczyk 1998). An obligatory motif on Tatar graves is a crescent with a star, placed at the top of the gravestone. This is a symbol of the revelation the Prophet Muhammad experienced at night, so the only witnesses to it were the moon and the stars (Olej-Kobus et al. 2009). Women are not allowed to participate in the burial, although, among contemporary Muslims in Poland, this restriction is not respected. Only earth burials are permitted. Cremation is prohibited in Islam. Mourning lasts for 40 days. For 40 days after the death, jasień or kurans for the soul of the deceased are recited, and on the 40th day the burial rites near the grave are repeated (Dziekan 2011; Kulikowski 2012). Visiting the Muslim graves at the All Saints is borrowed from the Christians (Kryczyński 2000; Dziekan 2011). The Polish followers of Islam don't light candles because their religion doesn't permit them to do so. They only place flowers and pray (Łyszczarz 2011).

The burial should take place immediately, on the same day or the following day after the death. Headwear is compulsory in the cemetery. No candles are lit at a Muslim cemetery, but it is traditional to burn a light in memory of the deceased at home. Candles can be seen on some graves, but this is the result of adopting Polish customs. There is no cremation or reuse of burial sites. Burials are in earthen graves. Kołodziejczyk (1998) gives a detailed description of the Muslim funeral rituals and the cult of the dead.

Poland is also home to followers of Eastern religions, including Buddhism (circa 12,150 believers) and Hinduism (circa 4,350 believers) (GUS 2022).

The Karaites are the smallest religious-ethnic minority in Poland (GUS 2019). The Polish name for those inhabiting Poland is *Karaimi*. They are descendants of the Crimean Karaites (of Turkish origin). Karaism (sometimes referred to as Karaite Judaism) emerged from Judaism in the 8th century (GUS 2022). According to the research of Wojciech Oleksiak (2015), the Karaites came to Poland and Lithuania at the turn of the 14th century (upon the invitation of the Grand Duke of Lithuania Vytautas). They are dispersed throughout the country. Followers of Karaism in Poland are affiliated with the Karaite Religious Union. Currently, the association is divided into three *jimats* (communes), with headquarters in Warszawa, Gdańsk and Wrocław. Poland's largest Karaite community is found in Warsaw. A detailed description of rituals connected with death, funerals, and mourning can be found in Mykolas Firkovičius's book (1999).

References

Act of 13 May 1994 on the Relationship of the State to the Evangelical-Augsburg Church in the Republic of Poland, JoL of 1994, No. 73, item. 323.

Borecki Paweł 2007, "Zasada równouprawnienia wyznań w prawie polskim" ("Principle of equality of religions in Polish law"), *Studia z Prawa Wyznaniowego*, Vol. 10, 115–159.

Bielawski Krzysztof, 2017, Ohele w Polsce z uwzględnieniem ich występowania na cmentarzach wielkomiejskich (Ohels in Poland with consideration of their occurrence in metropolitan cemeteries) [in:] Irmina Gadowska (ed.), Wielkomiejskie cmentarze żydowskie w Europie Środkowo-Wschodniej (Urban Jewish cemeteries in Central and Eastern Europe), Łódź. http://cmentarze-zydowskie.pl/ohele_w_polsce.pdf [10.05.2022]

CEC 2019, Conference of European Churches. https://ceceurope.org/ [10.05.2022]

Drembkowski Paweł 2018, Ustawa o cmentarzach i chowaniu zmarłych. Komentarz (Law on Cemeteries and Burial of the Dead. Commentary), Wydawnictwo C.H. Beck, Warszawa

Dziekan Marek M. 2011, *History and culture of Polish Tatars* (in:) Górak-Sosnowska K. (ed.), Muslims in Poland and Eastern Europe Widening the European Discourse on Islam, University of Warsaw Faculty of Oriental Studies Warszawa, 27–39.

Fiedorczuk Jan, Fiedorczuk Justyna, Fiedorczuk Irena 2013, *Death as a mystery. The funeral picture in The Eastern Orthodox Church* (in:) Krajewska-Kułak E., Guzowski A., Kułak W., Rozwadowska E., Łukaszuk C., Lewko

J. (eds.), Death education – the importance of medical care, Medical University of Białystok Faculty of Health Sciences, Białystok, 243–255.

Firkovičius Mykolas (ed.) 1999, Karaj dińliliarniń jalbarmach jergialiari. 2 bitik. Ochumach üčiuń adieť vahdalarynda, Vilnius

Gruber Samuel, Myers Phyllis 1995, *Survey of historic Jewish monuments in Poland: a report to the United States Commission for the Preservation of America's Heritage Abroad*, Jewish Heritage Council, World Monuments Fund, New York.

GUS 2019, Wyznania religijne w Polsce w latach 2015–2018 (Religious denominations in Poland 2015–2018), Warszawa.

GUS 2022, *Wyznania religijne w Polsce w latach 2019–2021* (Religious denominations in Poland 2019–2021), Warszawa.

Kołodziejczyk Arkadiusz 1998, *Cmentarze muzułmańskie w Polsce* (Muslim cemeteries in Poland), Ośrodek Ochrony Zabytkowego Krajobrazu, Narodowa Instytucja Kultury, Warszawa.

Kowalik Krzysztof 2010, *Religious and Cultural Potential of Protestantism in Catholic Poland* (in:) Kowalik K., Ulanowski K. (eds.), The role of religious minorities in functioning of the society of Gdańsk and the chosen European cities: the experiences of the past, contemporary days and the prognosis for the future, Instytut Kaszubski, Gdańsk, 43–51.

Krajewska-Kułak Elżbieta, Kułak Wojciech, Guzowski Andrzej, Kułak Piotr, Kułak Agnieszka, Bejda Grzegorz, Rozwadowska Emilia, Łukaszuk Cecylia, Lewko Jolanta, Van Damme-Ostapowicz Katarzyna, Cybulski Mateusz, Klimaszewska Krystyna, Kowalczuk Krystyna, Sierakowska Matylda 2013, *The symbolism of burial and cemeteries of Jehovah's Witnesses, sun worshipers, Buddhists, Karaite, Armenian, Lemko and secular* (in:) Krajewska-Kułak E., Guzowski A., Kułak W., Rozwadowska E., Łukaszuk C., Lewko J. (eds.), Death education – the importance of medical care, Medical University of Białystok Faculty of Health Sciences, Białystok, 579–600.

Kramer Kenneth Paul 2007, *Śmierć w różnych religiach świata* (Death in different world religions), WAM, Kraków.

Kryczyński Stanisław 2000, *Tatarzy litewscy. Próba monografii historyczno-etnograficznej* (The Lithuanian Tatars. Outline of a historical and etnographic monograph), Zakład Graficzny "Drukprasa".

Kubiak Anna E. 2015, *Pogrzeby to nasze życie* (Funerals are our lives), IFiS PAN, Warszawa.

Kulikowski Selim 2012, "Mizary – nekropolie mało znane. Tam, gdzie nie palono zniczy" (Mizars – little-known necropolises. Where no candles were burnt), *Memento. Dwumiesięcznik Funeralny*, No. 6, 35–37.

Łyszczarz Michał 2011, Generational changes among young Polish Tatars [in:] Górak-Sosnowska K. (ed.), Muslims in Poland and Eastern Europe Widening the European Discourse on Islam, University of Warsaw Faculty of Oriental Studies Warszawa, 53–68

Nalborczyk Agata, Borecki Paweł 2011, "Relations between Islam and the state in Poland: the legal position of Polish Muslims", *Islam and Christian – Muslim Relations*, 22(3), 343–359. 10.1080/09596410.2011.586514.

56   *Anna E. Kubiak and Anna Długozima*

Olej-Kobus Anna, Kobus Krzysztof, Rembas Michał 2009, *Nekropolie. Zabytkowe cmentarze wielokulturowej Polski* (Necropolies. Historic cemeteries of multicultural Poland), Carta Blanca, Warszawa.

Oleksiak Wojciech 2015. *The Disputed Origins of Poland's Smallest Ethnic Minority*. https://culture.pl/en/article/the-disputed-origins-of-polands-smallest-ethnic-minority [10.05.022].

Pasek Zbigniew 2020, "Kościoły i związki wyznaniowe we współczesnej Polsce: wykaz wraz z komentarzem" (Churches and religious organizations in contemporary Poland: the list along with commentary), *Przegląd Religioznawczy. The Religious Studies Review*, 2(276), 199–221.

Rogowska Barbara 2014, "Stanowisko władz komunistycznych w latach siedemdziesiątych XX wieku w zakresie cmentarnictwa wyznaniowego i komunalnego" (The position of the communist regime on the religious and communal cemeteries in the 1970s.), *Annales Universitatis Paedagogicae Cracoviensis Studia Politologica*, XIII, Folia 165, 75–93

Romanowicz Wiesław 2015, "Współczesne oblicze polskiego prawosławia" (Modern face of the Polish Orthodox Church), *Colloquium Wydziału Nauk Humanistycznych i Społecznych*, 3, 159–180.

Rykała Andrzej 2009, "Uwarunkowania geograficzno-polityczne oraz społeczne genezy i rozprzestrzeniania się protestantyzmu w Polsce" (Geopolitical and social determinants of origin and expansion of protestantism in Poland), *Acta Universitatis Lodziensis Folia Geographica Socio-Oeconomica*, 10, 61–87.

Warmińska Katarzyna 1999, *Tatarzy polscy. Tożsamość religijna i etniczna* (Polish Tatars. Religious and ethnic identity), Universitas, Kraków.

Washington Hebrew Congregation, A Guide for Jewish Funeral Practices, http://secure.whctemple.org/site/usermedia/application/7/guide-for-jewish-funeral-practices.pdf.

Wilczura Aleksandra 2010, "Śmierć i życie pozagrobowe w żydowskich wierzeniach ludowych" (The Death and Afterlife in Jewish folk beliefs), *Studia Bliskowschodnie*, 1(4), 34–41.

Worldmark Encyclopedia of Religious Practices 2015, 2nd Edition, Gale. https://corp.credoreference.com/component/booktracker/edition/11477.html [10.05.2022].

7 The Funeral Industry

Anna E. Kubiak

A General Characterization of Funeral Parlors in Poland

The dominant models of funeral parlors in Poland are the standard municipal model, where public enterprises (most of them were partly privatized after the 1990s) handle the funeral – and the commercial model, where control of the disposal of the dead is granted to private companies. In the 21st century private business has been the most prevalent. There are also funeral homes operated by officials of the local parish of the Catholic Church, but they are also commercial.

The Polish funeral industry is characterized by fragmentation and competitiveness. In small towns, there are a few parlors each, while large cities have a dozen or more. In Warsaw, there are about 200 funeral parlors. According to data from the REGON register, in 2019 there were 3,986 enterprises in Poland that declared they conducted a funeral business. Due to the merely declarative nature of the information provided to the REGON register, it should be assumed that the number of funeral companies actually operating on the funeral market is smaller. However, it is not possible to determine this precisely. "Industry organizations estimate that the number of actually operating companies providing funeral services is at a level of about 2,500" (Kolek, Lang, Kozłowski 2019, 21). The Polish funeral market is dominated by micro-enterprises. Establishments in the form of an individual business of a natural person prevail, while civil partnerships are in second place. On average, funeral companies employ fewer than ten people. "There are 134 funeral companies with between 10 and 49 employees, and 9 entities employ between 50 and 249 people" (Kolek, Lang, Kozłowski 2019, 21).

The Polish funeral market is based on the funeral allowance, the size of which is 4,000 PLN, which – as of mid-March, 2022 – is about 850 euros. This is a comparatively high allowance in Europe, although, in large urban areas where prices are higher (including the high cemetery space fee), 4,000 PLN is not enough to cover funeral costs. Not all

DOI: 10.4324/9781003207634-7

customers spend the whole funeral allowance on the funeral, but many of them spend much more.

> It should be pointed out, however, that on average funeral expenses are estimated at 8–10 thousand PLN (1710,40 – 2138,00 – AEK). This means that the funds actually flowing may be even twice as much as the funds coming from the funeral allowance and documented expenses for this purpose.
>
> (Kolek, Lang, Kozłowski 2019, 35)

In the evaluation of the funeral market, one must take into account the fragmentation of the funeral industry, and the division of the market between around 2,500 funeral homes. We also have to remember that the funeral industry in Poland started in the 1990s, and undertakers had to invest in their businesses.

Modern Funeral Establishment

The architecture of many funeral homes still resembles that of the Communist era. These buildings have the appearance of kiosks or commercial pavilions (Figure 7.1).

Some companies are in single-family homes, where the funeral facility occupies the first floor and the upper floors are occupied by the owner's family. A few business owners build modernistic funeral homes, with a

Figure 7.1 Funeral home in Warsaw. Photograph by Anna E. Kubiak.

Figure 7.2 Funeral home in Łódź. Photograph by Anna E. Kubiak.

parking lot in front of the funeral homes and, sometimes, a tombstone display (Figure 7.2).

Few undertakers, particularly those having a long family tradition (from before World War II), have adopted Western patterns. Such modern funeral homes include the whole infrastructure: reception rooms or one room with several workstations, a shop with coffins, urns, and bereavement clothes, a farewell chamber, an accounting, and human resources office, social facilities for the team leaving to bring the remains to the client, a warehouse, a room for storing the remains, a room dedicated to preparing the remains for burial, and a garage (Figure 7.3). Modern farewell chambers, in addition to a catafalque for the casket, a cross (which is removed in secular ceremonies), candlesticks, wreath stands, devotional items, and chairs for mourners, are equipped with a lectern and a screen for displaying photos and videos. Some funeral homes have rooms for families to confer over burial details. These establishments create a home-like atmosphere. The most successful establishments have their own florists, carpenters, bookstores, devotional stores, and coffee shops.

However, there are many funeral parlors – the so-called *bush firms* – which consist only of a small building for meetings with clients. All funeral products and services are presented in a catalog and are arranged after the contract with a client.

Presence in the Public Space

Funeral homes are most often located in "strategic places," that is, where people rub shoulders with death. First of all, these are buildings along

Figure 7.3 Reception desk in a funeral home in Łódź. Photograph by Anna E. Kubiak.

the streets running next to the cemetery. The vicinity of the registry office is a 'strategic place' due to the fact that death certificates are being processed there. The third such place – questionable from an ethical point of view – is the area around a hospital and/or hospice. They may be part of a string of downtown commercial pavilions.

The advertisements of funeral parlors are not only those characteristic of small companies, but they also include wall screens, billboards, e.g., at the Centrum subway station.

Through sponsorship of sports clubs and via charity, cultural events, and free funerals of famous people (accident victims), funeral marketing is created by giving the company's logo visibility. Other places of promotion are trade magazines, funeral fairs, and local press. Over the past 20 years, the Internet has become the most important place to advertise a business. Most parlors have a website with helpful information and documents for the families of the deceased. The most common phrases in advertising refer to the 24-hour on-call service and "comprehensive services"; i.e., the promise to take care of everything for the customer. The hearse is, according to undertakers, the funeral home's best showcase. The so-called "flagship hearse" means the most representative car, e.g., a Mercedes or, in the case of the most prosperous companies, a Jaguar, Chrysler, or Maserati (Kubiak 2015).

Necro-Business

The outdated law on cemeteries and burials, and the lack of adequate regulations regarding the requirements for funeral homes, have given rise to numerous pathologies. These include storing corpses in improper conditions, e.g., in garages or warehouses, improperly adapted vehicles for transporting corpses, inadequate sanitary and epidemiological safety procedures, "the grey market," and unfair competition. So-called *bush companies* engage in dumping – they reduce costs by informally hiring employees (they do not pay contributions toward employees' salaries) and illegally purchasing wood to produce coffins, which translates into lower funeral costs and reduced taxes. Extortionate extra charges by gravediggers for grave preparation are not uncommon (Kolek, Lang, Kozłowski 2019, 27–30).

Serious irregularities also relate to the presence of funeral home employees on hospital premises. The emissaries of some companies solicit families, knowing of someone's death (often by having paid hospital emergency workers and doctors for information about deaths), right in front of the hospital – some even advertise their services on hospital premises and hand out business cards. A big problem is the leasing of hospital prosectoriums by funeral homes, as some regions lack cold rooms and prosectoriums that should be mandatory for funeral homes to have. There are cases of illegal charging for the washing and dressing of corpses because no regulations clearly state which activities for preparing the deceased for burial belong to the hospital (free of charge) and which activities belong to the funeral home (when funeral services are prohibited on the premises of health care institutions). In other cases, the hospital decides for the family which funeral home they will choose.

References

Kolek Antoni, Lang Grzegorz, Kozłowski Łukasz 2019, *Branża pogrzebowa w Polsce* (Funeral industry in Poland), Centrum Analiz Legislacyjnych i Polityki Ekonomicznej, Warszawa.

Kubiak Anna E. 2015, *Pogrzeby to nasze życie* (Funerals are our lives), IFiS PAN, Warszawa.

8   The Funeral

Anna E. Kubiak

General Characteristics

Current funerals are usually lavish compared with, for example, funerals in Germany, the Czech Republic, or Great Britain. This is influenced by the role of social prestige. The funeral in Poland is an important family ritual that integrates family, professional, neighborhood, and friendship ties. The burial is a manifestation of the social status of the deceased and the wealth of the family (Ostrowska 1997, 225), as well as its religious denomination. Therefore – even if the deceased was a non-believer or a non-practicing Catholic – the family often chooses a religious ceremony.

There are local differences also, where customs are introduced by the funeral home and the priest of a particular parish. For example, it is up to the priest to approve a funeral vigil at the casket in the church, and a procession on foot. The latter custom is also influenced by the mayor of the town. There are clear differences between funerals in the countryside, those in small towns, and those in the big city. In the countryside, death is still a social event and this rite of passage is attended not only by the family but also by numerous neighbors. They are invited to the wake, which takes on the character of a large feast (60–100 people).

In the past, the wake was held at home, but nowadays it is organized in village common rooms, firehouses, and the like, where catering is ordered. In the city, a wake is usually held among the closest family, in a restaurant. In the countryside, it is more common to order an oak coffin with decorative fittings and lace lining on the outside. In the city it is not important what kind of wood the coffin is made of; only its appearance is important. In the countryside, secular and cremation funerals are only occasionally ordered, while in the city the number of cremations is increasing, and secular funerals have ceased to be something extraordinary (Kubiak 2015).

DOI: 10.4324/9781003207634-8

The Principal Components of a Funeral

The rite of burial consists of a series of more or less complex rites and operations. They differ according to the following factors: the place of death and its cause; the disposition of the body of the deceased; whether it is embalmed or not; the choice between burial in a grave or cremation; the relationship with a church (i.e., a religious or secular funeral); a mass with a coffin or an urn in the case of cremation, and, in the latter case, the ways of disposing of the ashes and the place of their burial. I will discuss here the fixed points of the funeral scenario – the ones characteristic of most burials.

After Death

If a person dies in a medical institution, there are procedures in place for declaring death, taking care of the deceased, and placing the body in cold storage. In the case of death at home, the doctor must be called to issue a death certificate and the family contacts the funeral home to take the body to a refrigerator. Next, the family must obtain an official death certificate from the registrar's office. Only then does the family go to the funeral home to prepare the stage for the funeral.

Funeral Arrangements

Mourners are usually received by a receptionist at the funeral home. Usually, this function is performed by women because of the reputation shared among funeral directors for feminine delicacy and tact. When the deceased had a high social status, then the business manager steps in. He or she also intervenes in unusual situations. For example, if the corpse has not been identified by the family when brought to the establishment (not all follow this rule), and the mourners are resistant to this operation, the receptionist may ask the manager to talk to them. If the family is still reluctant, they must sign a statement that they are taking legal and financial responsibility for the possible substitution of bodies when they are released for burial.

Through properly asked questions, the client's expectations are filtered through professional terms and formulated into the language of the funeral home in the form of a contract. The signing of a contract includes the cost of each service, the products purchased, and the timing of the service. Modern companies have an agreement signed with the Social Insurance Institution to obtain benefits on behalf of the family. The estimated time of the funeral is also specified, although it requires later arrangements with the administration of the church and the priest where the funeral service is to be held, the administration of the cemetery, possibly with the master of ceremonies, and the crematorium.

Artifacts

One of the most important and expensive artifacts is the coffin. Predominating in Poland are oak and pine coffins (about 50/50), generally lacquered in high gloss. The oak coffin is treated as a symbol of Polish funeral traditions. Its symbolism of durability and quality is important. The tradition of putting many private belongings of the deceased in the coffin is very widespread. I have noted the following items put in the coffin: crossword puzzle, pen, fur coat, glasses, hat, flask of vodka, rosary, favorite book, money, letters, guitar, tape recorder, skis, devotional book, cell phone, radio, newspapers, perfume, holy wreaths for the Blessed Virgin Mary, mirror, comb, walking stick, handkerchief, picture, cigarettes, Jagiellonia scarf for a deceased Jagiellonia fan, toys, mascots, laptop, samurai sword.

Artifacts most often ordered by the family are the coffin, a plaque, hourglasses, obituaries, flowers, and musical setting. Funerals in Poland usually include traditional wreaths. However, more ambitious florists, from "florist studios," draw their style from Western Europe, especially from Germany and Holland. From here came the fashion for wreaths, and from here come the dominant tones and styles; e.g., in 2004 for brown with greenery with a touch of pink, and to lighten the white and yellow, rustic style. Plaques play an important role in Polish burials, with the first name, surname, and date of death, or the number of years lived. They are placed on the grave among flowers or nailed to a wooden cross.

Humanizing the Corpse

In the funeral home, the process of the deceased becoming "our dearly departed" takes place: The corpse is subjected to *humanization*, as Howarth (1996, 147) calls the set of treatments and revitalization techniques by which the mortician restores a corpse's human face. This allows the mourners to see the deceased once again as she or he looked in life. This need celebrates the individuality of the deceased and their immortality in the sense of being stored in memory, surviving in the memories of posterity (Howarth 1996, 147).

Through proper coiffure, dress, and positioning in the coffin, not only is the corpse restored to the attributes of a human being, but it is festively prepared. At the same time, the face should be given a calm expression. The most important thing is the face and hands exposed in the ritual of the last farewell. The position of the body, the head on the pillow, and the coffin are to create the fiction that the deceased has fallen asleep. These procedures protect the mourners from contamination and odor, both physical and symbolic. The work of morticians includes washing, shaving, cutting nails, combing hair, curling rollers for women, arranging the body in a dignified pose, cosmetics, dressing, and placing in the coffin. Additionally, if so requested by the family, the body is embalmed. In Poland, embalming is performed on about 2% of the deceased. After accidents, the body has to be reconstructed.

Viewing the Deceased

In Poland, there is a very strong tradition of saying goodbye to the deceased, which often takes place in the chapel of the funeral home, but in the countryside and in small towns – especially on the eastern side of Poland – this ceremony often takes place at home, to which the coffin is brought one or more hours before the funeral. In the country and in small towns this is traditionally accompanied by rosary recitation and sprinkling of the body in the coffin by the priest. In the countryside, the last farewell is accompanied by many neighbors. In addition to its function of identifying the deceased, it is religious and emotional in nature. In contrast with the American ceremony, where the mortician has given the deceased a semblance of life, in Poland the deceased lies perpendicular to the family approaching him. This expresses a different attitude to the body of the deceased. In the United States, the family and friends approaching the body from the side of the deceased have a familiar and intimate relationship with him (Laderman 2003). In Poland, where they approach from the feet of the deceased, the relationship is one of reverence and homage to the body. In the cities, this ritual is compressed and limited to one hour before the funeral, and multimedia is sometimes used.

The Traditional Funeral Ceremony

When the removal of the deceased is traditionally done from the house, the procession goes to the *figurine*, which is the nearest roadside shrine or cross, where the congregants pray, and then the procession heads to the church. Another fixed point of a traditional burial is the funeral service in the church, to which the mourners and moribund are transported, while in the countryside and some small towns there is a walking procession, with the coffin being carried by hearse.

The funeral service is another regular feature of a traditional funeral. In the church, control of the ceremony is handed over to the other important director of the traditional funeral: the priest who conducts the funeral service.

After the end of the Mass, the officials (drivers and escorts) enter the church to efficiently lift the coffin and flowers and, with a dignified step, walk out to the cars. At the head of the procession stands the funeral or church assistants who carry a cross and sometimes flags, followed by the priest, then the coffin carried by the hearse, and then the mourners, with the closest relatives of the deceased in front. Depending on the distance between the church and the cemetery, the procession continues on foot or in cars.

At the Cemetery

On entering the cemetery, the church bells ring. Here the mourners may have some input into the ceremony in the form of speeches. The priest reciting the prayers plays an essential role. Musical settings have become an important part of burial. This is the most commonly performed funeral canon in the form of songs: *Ave Maria, Barka, Silence, Hello Queen*. Songs can be performed by musicians or played with recorded music on a sound system. It is extremely important that the coffin be smoothly lowered into the grave by the funeral assistants or local cemetery gravediggers. Some funeral parlors give guests a basket with small flowers to toss on the coffin to say goodbye to the deceased via this symbolic gesture. Technological solutions in the form of elevators and cemetery tents have emerged. The custom of not filling in a grave in front of guests has been adopted in many places. If there is a brick gravestone already standing, it is covered up as noiselessly as possible, and flowers and a plaque are placed on it. At the cemetery, or after the mourners have been dropped off at a restaurant, the funeral home staff discreetly moves away. Commemorative holy pictures with a prayer for the deceased and the details of the establishment have become popular: a sort of remembrance and business card of the company. Guests are left to themselves or (if so agreed) are driven to, for example, a restaurant, where a wake is held.

Funeral Meal

Family and friends integrate in this significant phase of the rite of passage. There must always be enough money for a wake at a traditional Polish funeral. The wake is a permanent part of the funeral scenario, which is why municipal cemeteries and funeral homes build halls on their premises for this purpose. A wake is dominated by Polish cuisine: broth, tripe, żurek (sour soup), schabowy (pork chops), and ribs spiked with vodka. At the wakes of people on Poland's eastern borderland, there appear Lithuanian cooler, kolduny, Russian dumplings, and kulebiakas.

After some time, the family will once again meet with funeral workers to settle the expenses: to pay extra or get back part of the funeral allowance. Some mourners pick up ordered photo essays or videos. On the anniversary of the death, some funeral parlors send the family a remembrance and order a Mass at their expense.

Polish Savoir Vivre at Funerals

Polish savoir vivre for behavior during funerals long remained very conservative: people dressed in black and widows came in hats with a black veil. The many people in attendance behaved very quietly, and all prayed along with the priest. However, since the 1990s, while in the countryside almost the entire community still goes to funerals, in the cities they are held within one's own family along with a few friends, neighbors, and possibly co-workers – unless the deceased was a well-known figure. Although some mourners still order wreaths (with flower bouquets dominating), there is no one to carry them, so this duty falls to funeral home workers. The tradition of mourning wear has also changed. Nowadays, people generally dress in dark clothes, but many people do not observe this. For example, men sometimes are seen wearing jeans with a jacket, maybe a t-shirt under the jacket, and sneakers – while women wear dresses with frills and necklines.

Differences Between the Village and the City

There are differences between the village and the city. One of them concerns the rite of vigil, which is held at the funeral home. In the village, it is customary to approach the coffin first, to stand in silence or speak to the deceased, and to kiss him/her or touch his/her hand. One approaches from the side of the deceased's feet; the intercourse is reverent and pays homage to the body. The rosary and other prayers for the soul are recited. In the morning, from eight o'clock on the day of a funeral, they come again until the priest arrives.

It's different in the city, where multimedia is used instead of the rosary. Mourners come only once, on the day of the funeral, and pray or simply indulge in contemplation, with music that reaches them quietly from the back of these chapels. There are masters of ceremonies (MCs) who, depending on the expectations of particular families, suitably adapt the event. For instance, the MCs may reminisce on the basis of passages from the biography of the deceased, as previously agreed with the family. The funeral parlor owner records photos or texts on CDs and displays them in the chapel. People gather around the open coffin, they sit on benches or chairs, and they gaze at the pictures of the deceased at different times in his or her life.

In villages, there must always be enough money for a feast, where up to 150 people participate. Whereas in the past this was performed at the mourners' home, now catering is ordered and delivered to community centers, such as fire stations. Undertakers say, "They bargain for a coffin, but a wake for at least 70 people has to be held to give a decent burial". In the city, a funeral meal is held in the close circle of the immediate family, in a restaurant. Thus, while in the city the funeral involves a narrow circle, in the countryside death is still a social event, and a funeral feast is attended not only by family but also by many neighbors. It strengthens family, neighborhood, work, and friendship ties. It lasts longer in villages and includes the whole community, although today holding the feast in a house is usually excluded, as the feast takes place in the public sphere. Contemporary urban funeral rites of passage are compressed and limited to personal bereavement.

Economic Differences

Funerals are a reflection of the deepening diversification of citizens' wealth. Establishments' ability to provide a wide range of offerings influences the diversification of funerals according to wallet wealth and social hierarchy. The deceased obtains socioeconomic status through the choice of clothing, the type of coffin, decorum in the form of artifacts such as the number and magnificence of the wreaths, a photo plaque, a multimedia show dedicated to their life, a hired trumpeter, violinist or a whole orchestra, an elegant hearse, the feast in their honor, and a gravestone.

Burials can be within the limits of the funeral allowance, but can also amount to tens of thousands of złoties and more. For example, one can order a coffin made of tropical wood, with natural silk lining, specially imported from abroad, for fifteen thousand dollars. In case it turns out that someone in a comatose state was put in the grave by mistake, a small radio transmitter kept by the family is put inside. If something unpredictable were to happen, it would immediately pick up the signal. Even the slightest sign of life automatically opens the compressed oxygen container mounted in the coffin.

Humanistic Ceremony

There are no data for estimating the number of secular funerals in Poland, but only rough estimates from MCs themselves. They estimate that secular funerals in Poland, taking place predominantly in large cities, amount to about 5% of all burials. Because of growing demand, some big-city funeral homes appoint one of their employees to serve in this capacity. There are more than 20 masters of ceremonies, but only six are experienced and have specialized in lay ceremonial for years.

Humanist funerals are individualistic in nature and oriented toward the life of the deceased. The rite is primarily a ceremony for the mourners. A solemn farewell to a relative allows the mourner to find a relationship with the deceased that is a lasting bond and can be uplifting (Walter 2001).

A humanist ceremony may be part of a religious funeral with all the repertoire of a traditional inhumation: a Mass and prayer by a priest in a cemetery. It may also be that the religious part is limited to the presence of a priest at the cemetery. Sometimes the MCs themselves lead the prayer. This is why some officiants protest against referring to the rite they celebrate as secular. Still another form is the secular funeral.

Although this form of officiant has existed for many years, in Poland there are no regulations concerning the dress and duties of the master of ceremonies or for the script of the ritual. There is also no official certification of this profession. In Poland, each of the celebrants has their own individual style of conducting the ceremony, according to their own dress design and their own vision of the rite of passage. Some of the longest-serving officiants perform in black togas in the 13th-century style of the doctor's toga trimmed with a bright yellow plastron, wearing white gloves, and on cold days wearing a black velvet beret. Another officiant designed and ordered from a tailor an outfit consisting of a black tailcoat with gray piping, a black hat, and white gloves (used at the beginning of the ceremony) and black gloves (worn on the way to the cemetery). Other, long-time masters dress in a black toga and wear a tie and a chain around their neck with the city's emblem – for example, the mermaid, if the ceremony is held in Warsaw. There are masters who wear ordinary clothes suitable for a funeral; for example, a black coat or a dark suit.

The master begins his work by speaking with the family, either at an appointment or, sometimes, by phone. Together with the mourners, the life of the deceased and the scenario of the ceremony are discussed. The main task of the master of ceremonies is to prepare a farewell speech centered around the life of the deceased. The relatives decide what should be included in the memoir of the deceased and the musical repertoire. In addition, the script of the ceremony depends on whether the ceremony begins in the funeral home, in the farewell hall, or in the cemetery, and on the number of people who want to give a eulogy.

Beyond the Framework of Tradition

There are also generational changes in the attitude toward funerals. Contemporary young people want a liberalization of the cemetery law in order to allow the scattering of ashes in the favorite places of the deceased, ecological cemeteries, and green burials. Already today, about 5% of ashes are not buried at the cemetery. People scatter them – illegally for now – according to the will of the deceased. Though practiced, it is illegal to take ashes home in the reliquaries sold by funeral homes. Young people think about personal, individual burials not only for themselves but also for their relatives. The owners of funeral homes recognize the demand for other forms of rites of passage, although they are often considered quaint. Above all, these funerals are organized in

large metropolitan areas. In small towns and villages, a family organizing an alternative burial could face social ostracism. Funeral directors
pay particular attention to new music ordered at the funeral, and include
"disco polo" songs. The individualization of funerals can be seen in
the author's urn designs. They express a departure from the cliché and
propose an artistic expression of the rite of passage. The new funeral
fashion of putting a photo next to the coffin gives the funeral a more
individual character.

A move away from the baroque character of Polish funerals and
the promotion of greater simplicity, along with ecological qualities,
is also evident among some manufacturers. Wicker coffins with linen
decor, although made primarily for export, are offered by a Polish
company. A production plant sewing linen shrouds has appeared.
All these "expressive" values are also increasingly evident in floral
design – artistic bouquets that are smaller than standard wreaths.
To date, the percentage of alternative burials is small. The most ex-
travagant funerals were offered by an establishment in Koszęcin,
founded by enthusiasts of thanatology and goth culture and referred
to in the media as "the Addams family". Thus, they aroused protests
from locals, and the owners emigrated to Great Britain. A family in
Bielsko-Biała, after the cremation of a relative, moved the headstone
away themselves to preserve the urn. There is also a growing demand
for new forms of funeral commemoration, including professional
photographs.

Funeral planning services are entering the market, albeit with resistance, and hence are currently confined to the margins. Poles still rely on
the state funeral allowance and do not want to accumulate savings
for the funeral, so the funeral insurance offered by some establishments
is not accepted. This requires changes in the law. Planning one's own
funeral may influence the evolution of funerals toward more individualistic, thematic, alternative rituals.

These new ideas are being popularized by the Good Death Institute
(GDI). The GDI was founded in 2020 as a grassroots community initiative, and for its first two years, it operated as an informal association.
In 2022 it became a non-profit company. The goal of the GDI is to raise
public awareness and provide education about dying and bereavement,
and new, personal forms of funerals.

In 2021 the community initiative (Un)forgotten Cemeteries drafted
the new "Law on Cemeteries and Funerals". The project tables the
possibility of new forms of burial: the practice of scattering ashes from
cremation in Memorial Gardens in cemeteries, on private land after
gaining the owner's consent, and on public land (local government,
state) without consent, with the exclusion of certain places (such as

inland waters and the sea at a certain distance from the coast), and green burials. This new bill has yet to proceed to Parliament.

New Technologies

In Poland, funeral homes have begun to introduce new technologies, such as lifts for coffins, software for funeral budgeting, and "memory diamonds"' created from ashes or a lock of hair. Cemetery administrators have developed electronic cemetery maps, an online search engine, and photo codes with which – after scanning an image on the wall of a cemetery chapel with one's phone – one uses an application to type in the name of the deceased to find the grave. Another company has developed *quar codes* placed on a piece of granite and mounted on a tombstone. By touching the monument with an NFC-enabled smartphone, an internet connection is made to a database containing genealogical and biographical information about the deceased, along with photos. So far, orders have come mainly from Italy, Hungary, the USA, Israel, and Australia. Polish customers' lack of interest is perhaps influenced by the phenomenon of "cemetery hyenas" (robbers).

The region of Dolny Śląsk (Lower Silesia) is the most modern Polish funeral market, and one example of this is its Memorial Park funeral home in Ruda Śląska. Inspired by a Canadian innovation, it offers funeral performances in which a coffin, open or closed, is placed on a moving cylinder (which acts as a catafalque) that spins around an axis while moving across space. Meanwhile, the multimedia room provides high-quality music, changing lighting, and projected film or slides. Finally, the coffin – controlled by a director hidden behind Venetian glass – moves the cylinder toward the door to the crematorium vestibule, where it exits the room, and then the door silently closes.

Funerals of Motorcyclists

Classified in modern thanatology as *themed* funerals, ceremonies characterized by an appropriate selection of funeral accessories and rituals related to the profession or passion of the deceased, are a kind of folklore, particularly for the burials of motorcyclists. On the online forums of *motonites* (which is what motorcyclists call themselves as opposed to *tinkers* – car drivers), notification is posted about the death and funeral of a colleague. The funeral rally is attended by a dozen to several dozen machine enthusiasts, who often do not personally know the deceased. Tributes to the deceased are paid by motorcyclists in black studded leather, and the procession (arranged by the mortician with the police) goes to the chapel (if the funeral liturgy element is observed) and later to the cemetery. Cremation is a common element, while ashes in an urn are carried on the saddle of a motorcycle. Harleys enter the cemetery – with the permission of the administration – to play a kind of funeral march: *przegazówka* (the roar of engines and the sounding of horns) at the final farewell, when the urn or coffin is lowered into the grave. At the end, the motorcycles burn rubber and peel out.[1]

Funerals and Cemeteries of Animals

Animal cemeteries in Poland[2] began to emerge in the second half of the 20th century. For many years, animals were buried illegally outside cities, in forests and allotments, in city parks, or turned over to veterinarians for disposal. In 1991, Poland's first pet cemetery, "Dog's Destiny" near Warsaw, was opened. Prices for burials there vary between 500 and 800 zloties. Several thousand creatures are already buried on its grounds. This was followed by cemeteries in Szymanów near Wroclaw ("Rainbow Bridge"), in Piła ("Pet Meadow"), in Rzędziany near Białystok ("Small Animal Cemetery"), and in Ropczyce in southeast Poland ("Border"). Currently, there are 16 such cemeteries. Szymanów was the site of the first animal crematorium, of which there are now eight. The caregiver can bid the pet a solemn farewell, be present during incineration in the room where the furnace is located, he/she can observe the individual incineration of one pet, and collect the urn with ashes.

Nowadays one can buy the entire funerary assortment for a dignified burial of the animal: coffin, urn, headstone, plaque, candles, and flowers. On the Sunday closest to the feast of St. Francis – the patron saint of animals – the Animal Day of the Dead is celebrated. As in a human cemetery, caretakers refresh the graves – cleaning the slabs, lighting candles, and laying flowers. Photographs of animals are often placed on the slabs, along with their names and birth and death dates. However, in contrast to human cemeteries, the animal cemetery is cheerful in its decoration, with balloons and colorful pinwheels spinning by the graves, and on the slabs there are toys, ceramic figurines of animals, teddy bears, hearts, collected chestnuts, pine cones, and nuts.

The funeral is held in the presence of the immediate family, who make prior arrangements with a local mortician. The animal is often brought wrapped in a favorite blanket. Toys and food are also placed in the grave. Before the grave pit is filled, there is a moment for a final farewell. After that, the family shares memories of their pet. There are some people who say prayers. Some families hold a wake after the funeral (Figures 8.1 and 8.2).

Figure 8.1 Animal grave in Konik Nowy during the Animal Day of the Dead.
    Photograph by Anna E. Kubiak.

Figure 8.2 Animal grave in Konik Nowy during the Animal Day of the Dead.
Photograph by Anna E. Kubiak.

Notes

1 *Memento* 2006, 1, 17–19; *Memento* 2007, 6, 36.
2 A horse cemetery has been found in Poland in Kliczków near Bolesławiec, on the grounds of an 18th-century German palace. The preserved obelisks have the horses' names and dates of birth engraved on them (*Kultura Pogrzebu* 2006, 8, 19).

References

Howarth Glennys 1996, *Last rites. The work of the modern funeral director*, Baywood Publishing Company, Amityville, New York.
Kubiak Anna E. 2015, *Pogrzeby to nasze życie* (Funerals are our lives), IFiS PAN, Warszawa.
Kultura Pogrzebu 2012, 8, 19.
Laderman Gary 2003, *Rest in Peace. A cultural history of death and the funeral home in twentieth-century America*, Oxford University Press, Oxford.
Memento 2006, 1, 17–19.
Memento 2007, 4, 11.
Memento 2007, 6, 36.
Ostrowska Antonina 1997, *Śmierć w doświadczeniu jednostki i społeczeństwa* (Death in the experience of the individual and socjety), IFiS PAN, Warszawa.
Walter Tony 2001, "Sekularyzacja" (Secularization), in: Parkes C., Laungani P., Young B. (eds.), *Przemijanie w kulturach. Obyczaje żałobne, pocieszenie i wsparcie* (Passing in Cultures. Mourning customs, consolation and support), Astrum, Wrocław, 232–261.

9   Funeral Costs

Anna Długozima

The Costs of Funeral Services

As Monika Lewandowicz-Machnikowska (2015) emphasizes, funeral expenses are directly related to the funeral, and include storage and transportation of the body, preparation of the body for the funeral (cosmetics, embalming, clothing), incineration, purchase of a coffin or urn and other funeral accessories, preparation of the burial site (shaping of the grave, excavation and possible walling of the grave, and back-filling), conducting the funeral ceremony, and musical setting.

Average Prices

The cost of a funeral in Poland depends largely on where the ceremony is held. Prices in large cities such as Warsaw, Kraków, or Wrocław are usually much higher than those in smaller towns. The cost of a funeral consists of the basic and additional costs of funeral service, listed in Table 9.1. The total cost of a traditional funeral ranges from PLN 6700.00 to PLN 18000.00 (from EUR 1400.00 to 3900.00), EUR 2000.00 on average, while the total cost of a cremation funeral is about EUR 1700.00. Because cremation is cheaper than a traditional burial by, on average, 15–20%, the impact of this is a lower total cost.

The cost of cremation in Poland varies regionally and fluctuates between PLN 700 and 1100.

In Poland there is no insurance in case of a funeral, so all costs are covered from the funeral benefit or the family's own resources. As Krzysztof Wolicki, President of the Polish Funeral Association (2018), points out:

the current funeral benefit (ZUS funeral payment) of PLN 4000.00 is grossly low. In large cities, especially in the Warsaw, it does not even cover half of the costs of a traditional burial, which should be

DOI: 10.4324/9781003207634-9

Table 9.1 Price list of funeral services in Poland, with division of costs into
basic and additional (as of February 2023). Own elaboration based
on https://kb.pl/ and Omega (2020)

Category	Price range in PLN
Basic costs	
Corpse pick-up and transport	300–450
Preparation of the body for the funeral	330–560
Burial organization (transport by hearse, funeral procession, putting the coffin down into the grave, covering the grave)	2300–3500
Direct cremation (incineration in a crematorium)	840–1200
Cremation casket	400–800
Office fees	350–600
Funeral mass (conducting of the funeral by a priest)	840–1400
Secular funeral (conducting of the funeral by a celebrant)	800–1000
Additional costs	
Coffin	750–4700
Urn	200–2000
Musical setting (music services)	530–810
Flower decorations (wreath, flowers)	200–600
Storing the body in the cold store	110–170
Photographer (photographic documentation of the ceremony)	300–600
Consolation (price per person)	60–180
Single tombstone	from 5500
Double tombstone	from 8700

available to every citizen. According to that, funeral benefit does not fulfil the purpose for which it was established.

Currently, the funeral benefit covers an average of 40–50% of expenditure on a traditional burial and 100% of cremation costs – with regard to the above-mentioned statement.

There are also noticeable differences in the average costs of a secular funeral and one held in a religious rite (see Table 9.2).

It should be also emphasized that in the face of rising inflation, fuel, and electricity prices, it is becoming increasingly difficult for funeral parlors to maintain their former funeral service rates, especially as the Covid-19 outbreak made it mandatory for undertakers to use protective measures (e.g., masks, disinfectant fluids). An increase in the price of components for the manufacture of funeral accessories has also been recorded. In view of the above, an estimated increase of 20% will be recorded in relation to the rates presented above.

Table 9.2 Comparison of the cost of traditional and secular burial without the cost of a tombstone. Own elaboration based on Kubiak (2015, 138)

Costs	Traditional (religious) funeral (PLN)	Secular funeral (PLN)
Coffin	1385.00	695.00
Transport, transport by hearse	345.00	460.00
Putting the coffin down into the grave	80.00	300.00
Obituaries	50.00	90.00
Storing the body in the cold store	220.00	
Preparation of the body for the funeral	310.00	
Plaque on grave	55.00	54.20
Corpse pick-up	295.00	140.00
Flower decorations	930.00	390.00
Fee for burial site	The family owns burial site	100
Enlarging the grave	700.00	
Church fees	250.00	
Conducting the funeral	500.00 (priest)	350.00 (celebrant)
Funeral setting (e.g., musical services)	425.00	200.00 (trumpet over the grave)
Bricking up the grave		800.00
Funeral organization (office fees)	150.00	160.00
Total costs	**7045.00**	**3739.20**

The Funeral Benefit

In order to provide funds to the family of the deceased to cover funeral expenses, a funeral benefit is granted under the Polish social security system. Funeral benefit payments made by the Social Insurance Institution in Poland (ZUS) come from an annuity fund set aside as part of the Social Insurance Fund. In Poland, a funeral benefit is payable in the event of the death of an insured person, a retired person, a disabled pensioner, members of their families, and persons who have fulfilled the conditions for a pension. Eligible family members are the spouse (widow and widower), parents, stepfather, stepmother and adoptees, the deceased's own children, children of the spouse, adopted children and children placed in a foster family, other children adopted for upbringing and maintenance before reaching the age of majority, siblings, grandparents, grandchildren, persons over whom legal guardianship has been established. The funeral grant is also awarded in respect of the death of the insured person after the end of insurance if the death occurred during the period of receiving the sickness allowance, rehabilitation benefit, or maternity allowance.

The funeral payment is a one-off payment and is granted to persons or entities that have covered the funeral costs. If funeral costs were incurred by a family member of the deceased, he/she is entitled to the grant in full amount. It is not important what the actual expenses were. On the other hand, if funeral costs were covered by a non-family member (e.g., neighbor, employer) or an entity (e.g., a social welfare facility, municipality, county, legal person, church, or religious association), the funeral grant is payable in the amount of documented funeral costs up to a maximum of PLN 4000. If the costs were incurred by several persons or entities, the funeral grant is divided among them in proportion to their share. The funeral benefit is paid as standard by the Social Insurance Institution, in the case of farmers by the Agricultural Social Insurance Fund (KRUS), and in the case of police officers by the Pension Institution of the Ministry of Internal Affairs and Administration (MSWiA). In the case of working people, a one-off death allowance from their employer is also paid to the family of the deceased, independently of the death benefit. This is not a fixed amount and depends on the length of service. If the length of service was less than ten years, the employer pays the family one month's salary. When an employee worked between ten and fifteen years, three months' salary is applied, and for service of at least fifteen years, the death allowance is six months' salary.

The cemetery and funeral trade was materially impacted, and the interest in cremation was enhanced, by a reduction in funeral payments made by the ZUS, from PLN 6395 (ca. EUR 1500) to just under PLN 4000 in March 2011. Due to the fact the nominal value of the benefit has been kept stable, in real terms, its value is gradually decreasing on account of inflation. A funeral benefit of PLN 4000 currently translates into approximately EUR 840 (the Euro's exchange rate in December 2022).

Social Funerals

The provision of a funeral is one of the municipality's own tasks, which means that it is one of the benefits provided by social assistance. The municipality (competent for the place of death) is obliged to hold a funeral if:

- The deceased was uninsured, but also his or her next of kin are without work and without insurance, and the right of burial is relinquished by the next of kin and no other person (e.g., employer) or religious community declares a willingness to arrange the funeral (according to the law, burial may be carried out by any person who voluntarily undertakes to do so).

- No public university carrying out teaching and research activities in the field of medical sciences submits an application for the release of a corpse for scientific purposes (Cemeteries and Burials of the Deceased Act, Article 10).

In addition, the Act of 12 March 2004 on social assistance states that it is the responsibility of the municipality to provide funerals for homeless people and people of undetermined identity. This is handled on behalf of the municipality by social welfare centers. However, the municipality is entitled to compensation from, among other things, a funeral allowance if the deceased is entitled to one. If this is not the case, the municipality can be satisfied from the deceased's estate, if he or she left one (Grodziska 2019). The funeral arrangements are made in a manner determined by the municipality and in accordance with the deceased's religion. The cost of a funeral organized by the assistance center is lower than market prices, as funeral services are contracted by the municipality through an open tender for three-year periods. The average cost of a funeral is PLN 2000–2500, for funeral services (ca. PLN 1000) and cemetery fees, depending on the type of burial. In summation, the idea of social funerals in Poland is dedicated to the homeless, nameless (*nomen nescio*), and people with low incomes (Franczyk 2017).

Cemetery Costs

This subsection will characterize the costs of cemetery services. Cemetery services consist of organizing and supervising work related to:

- Maintaining the cemetery and equipping it with necessary facilities and devices.
- Arranging the cemetery in accordance with the development plan and providing access to cemetery infrastructure (communication routes, burial sites).
- Architectural and urban planning, sanitation, and ordering supervision over the use of the cemetery, including the burial, exhumation, erection of monuments, the establishment of graves in accordance with the law, and maintenance of cemetery books.

According to the report by the NIK (2016), the lack of a uniform catalog of fees for cemetery services and the varied method of calculating fees

Table 9.3 List of burial costs (as of April 2022). Own elaboration based on price lists valid in 20 selected cemeteries in Poland.

Scope of activities	Price range (gross value in PLN)
Fee for use of community property in connection with the performance of a funeral	400–600
Fee for marking out a burial site and supervising preparation of a grave	100–220
Gravedigging,* backfilling, grave shaping	300–600
Gravedigging, backfilling with border, grave shaping	650–800
Grave excavation, backfilling, grave shaping in winter, additional fee	70–100
Dredging of a grave	200–300
Restoration fee (placement of an urn or coffin in a masonry grave)	50 –250
Exhumation (to deepen a grave from a masonry grave, or from an earth grave)	500–1500
Bricking up the grave	500–1100
Placing a plaque on a grave with name, surname, and date of birth and death	50 –150
Removal of flowers and wreaths after the funeral	70–100

Notes
* The price is influenced by the type of grave: single-level or two-level (deep). The price is higher for deep graves.

adopted in municipalities fosters, on the one hand, a high degree of freedom in setting cemetery fees and, on the other hand, no allowance for comparison and evaluation of the method of calculating fee rates.

Costs associated with the burial of the deceased include digging and filling in the grave (see Table 9.3).

One of the first expenses incurred is the purchase of a burial place in the chosen cemetery, which is regulated by the administrative authorities of the cemetery. Purchase of the cemetery plot, according to the provisions of the Cemeteries and Burials of The Deceased Act, is for 20 years. This Act also mandates that masonry graves for two or more bodies are purchased in perpetuity.

The final cost is influenced by the location of the cemetery, the grave, and the size of the grave, among other factors. Burial sites located in historic cemeteries and in the centers of large cities are more expensive. In addition, there is an administration fee that fluctuates between PLN 400 and 1200 and is valid for 20 years. The fee is spent on the day-to-day upkeep of the cemetery (maintenance of greenery, waste disposal, cleaning, repairs, snow clearance, etc.) (see Table 9.4).

Table 9.4 List of costs for burial site (as of April 2022). Own elaboration based on price lists valid in 20 selected cemeteries in Poland.

Scope of activities	Price range (gross value in PLN)
Fee for providing a grave site for an earth grave for a period of 20 years (child, single, single- or double-level)	450–1300
Fee for providing a place for a masonry grave for a period of 20 years (single, double, single- or double-level)	1600–3000
Fee for a grave space (1-seat, 2-seat)	8700–12000
Fee for a coffin niche in a catacomb for a period of 20 years	1500
Fee for the provision of a coffin niche in an urn grave for a period of 20 years	500–1000
Fee for the provision of an urn niche in a columbarium for 20 years	1350–4500
Renewal fee* for an urn niche in a columbarium	500–1500
Renewal fee* for a ground-level grave (single, single- or double-level)	350–1000
Renewal fee* for a ground-level grave (double one- or two-level)	1000–1500

Notes
* Payment for the lease of the cemetery site after 20 years for a further 20 years.

The prices of tombstones will depend on the material used, the quality of workmanship, and the size. The average cost of a single tombstone ranges from PLN 5500.00 to PLN 7900.00. While the average cost of a double tombstone is PLN 8700.00 to 12100.00.

References

Franczyk Adam 2017, "Pochówek nomen nominandum" (Nomen nominandum burial), *Memento. Dwumiesięcznik Funeralny*, 4, 16–19.

Grodziska Beata 2019, "Sprawienie pochówku przez gminę w świetle orzecznictwa sądów administracyjnych" (Conducting a burial by the commune in the light of the judicature of administrative courts), S*tudenckie Prace Prawnicze, Administratywistyczne i Ekonomiczne*, 28, 221–234.

Kubiak Anna E., 2015, *Pogrzeby To Nasze Życie* (Funerals Are Our Lives), IFIS PAN, Warszawa.

Lewandowicz-Machnikowska Monika 2015, "Zasiłki pogrzebowe i inne świadczenia na pokrycie kosztów pogrzebu i upamiętnienia osoby zmarłej" (Death grants and other allowances aiming at covering of funeral and commemoration costs) (in:) Gołaczyński J., Mazurkiewicz J., Turłukowski J., Karkut D. (eds), *Non omnis moriar: osobiste i majątkowe aspekty prawne śmierci człowieka: zagadnienia wybrane*, Oficyna Prawnicza Uniwersytetu Wrocławskiego, Wrocław, 554–566 https://www.repozytorium.uni.wroc.pl/dlibra/publication/79431/edition/77872?language=pl [12.04.2022].

NIK 2016, *Zarządzanie cmentarzami komunalnymi* (Management of municipal cemeteries). https://www.nik.gov.pl/plik/id,12230,vp,14613.pdf [12.04.2022].

Omega, 2020, Raport branżowy. Industry report, *Magazyn Omega. Idea book dla branży pogrzebowej*, No. 1, 10–14.

Wolicki Krzysztof 2018, *Petycja w sprawie podwyższenia kwoty zasiłku pogrzebowego do wysokości 6000 zł* (Petition to increase the amount of funeral benefit to PLN 6000). https://www.polskiestowarzyszeniepogrzebowe.pl [12.04.2022].

10   Cemeteries, Burial Sites, and Graves

Anna Długozima

Current State of Cemeteries

There is no central database aggregating information on cemeteries in Poland. The last comprehensive statistical study with data about cemeteries in Poland, *Information on Cemeteries and War Graves*, covers the year 1969. GUS annually collects data about green areas, including cemeteries. However, GUS defines a cemetery as a place for the burial of the dead (human or animal) regardless of the legal status, owner/manager, or size of the area with greenery.

According to the GUS, as of 22 July 2021, there were 16,373 cemeteries in Poland. Their total acreage was 18,677.93 hectares. In 2021, most cemeteries were located in the countryside (13,483 cemeteries, 83% of the total). There were 2,890 cemeteries in the cities (17% of the total number of cemeteries). Every major city has a municipal cemetery, as opposed to rural areas where there are denominational cemeteries, especially parish ones (Długozima 2020).

Due to current legislation, there are two types of cemeteries in Poland: civil cemeteries, which serve the purpose of burying civilians, and military cemeteries, serving as burial places for soldiers. War cemeteries are subject to the provisions of the Act of 28 March 1933 on war graves and cemeteries. In turn, the Cemeteries and Burials of The Deceased Act regulates the planning and operation of civil cemeteries, distinguishing between two types: religious (denominational) and municipal (Drembkowski 2018).

Municipal Cemeteries

Municipal cemeteries are facilities that have been established by local authorities and have not been granted to the competent church/religious authority and that are maintained and managed by the competent voyt/ mayors/presidents. Municipal cemeteries may be established for several municipalities. Currently, 1,920 cemeteries in Poland have the status of

DOI: 10.4324/9781003207634-10

municipal facility, representing 12% of the total number of cemeteries (according to GUS data). PSP estimates that there are circa 3,000 municipal cemeteries. The report by the NIK (2016) pointed out many problems regarding the management of municipal cemeteries in Poland as well as some socio-cultural factors that determine the modern condition of burial facilities (progressing secularization, imitation of Western solutions). This report predicts that the share of municipal cemeteries in Poland will increase.

The spatial distribution of municipal cemeteries in Poland is unequal. As a result of geopolitical changes after WWII, many denominational cemeteries lost their users. In the period from the 1970s to the 1990s they were communalized and, nowadays, they are the property of local governments (Dziobek-Romański 1998, Rogowska 2014, NIK 2016, Długozima 2022).

The group of unusual municipal Polish cemeteries includes both historical and contemporary ones. Historical municipal cemeteries represent high artistic, compositional, and landscape values: the Central Cemetery in Szczecin; Rakowicki Cemetery in Kraków (see Figure 10.1); Osobowicki and Grabiszyński Cemeteries in Wrocław; Cemetery of Merit at Pęksowy Brzyzek in Zakopane; and a forest cemetery in the place of former gardens of Ignacy Krasicki in Lidzbark Warmiński.

Figure 10.1 Rakowicki Cemetery in Kraków is an example of a municipal cemetery. Photograph by Anna Długozima.

Contemporary municipal cemeteries prove that communal cemeteries designed in the second half of the 20th century and in the 21st century can be attractive: the Municipal Cemetery in Częstochowa; Northern Cemetery in Warsaw; and Southern Cemetery in Antoninów. The largest necropolis in Poland and the third-largest in Europe is the Central Cemetery in Szczecin. Moreover, one of the most beautiful collections of historic tombstones can be seen at this cemetery.

Religious Cemeteries

Churches and other religious organizations in Poland have the right to possess and establish religious cemeteries. They represent the oldest category of burial sites. Religious cemeteries may be established by all religious associations. With regard to religious associations whose legal situation is regulated by separate laws, the basis for the establishment of cemeteries shall be those laws and, with regard to the Catholic Church, also the Concordat. On the other hand, religious associations that do not have their legal situation regulated by law may operate cemeteries on the basis of the Act on the Guarantees of the Freedom of Conscience and Faith (1989).

A religious necropolis is owned by a parish and administered by a parish priest, who may delegate the administration thereof to other persons or entities. In places with a Roman Catholic parish cemetery only, its administrator should allow dead persons of other religions or non-believers, formerly resident in this parish, to be buried there. The Supreme Court of Poland stated that religious cemeteries are public-use facilities designed to meet the needs of followers of a particular religion for the burial of remains. However, they differ from municipal cemeteries in that their primary purpose is to bury the remains of deceased persons who belonged to a given religion and to perform religious rites. In towns where there are no municipal cemeteries, the management of a religious cemetery (parish priest) is obliged to allow the burials in such a cemetery without any discrimination, of deceased persons of other religions, or non-believers (Starzecka 2014).

According to the NID (Narodowy Instytut Dziedzictwa – National Heritage Board of Poland) report (2017), cemeteries account for 6.77% of the monuments in Poland. In the group of historical cemeteries, those owned by churches and religious associations dominate (over 70%). Roman Catholic cemeteries are in the best condition, while the group of endangered objects mostly concerns cemeteries of other denominations. A generally poor condition is characteristic of Jewish and Greek-Catholic cemeteries, while the most advanced state of neglect is found in Evangelical cemeteries (Lutheran, Calvinist) (Sobotka, Długozima 2015). There is a lack of up-to-date data on the number of religious

Table 10.1 Approximate number of religious cemeteries in Poland, as of 1994.
Own elaboration based on Michałowski (1995)

	Lutheran	Calvinist	Jewish	Catholic
Total number	7500	500	1000	19000
Historical	3000	100	300	6000
Well-kept	5%	5%	30%	60%

cemeteries. The last such compilations date back to the 1980s and 1990s, when systematic documentation and records of garden layouts and cemeteries in Poland were carried out. Michałowski (1995), at an international symposium dedicated to cemetery art, reported that Poland has a religiously diverse sepulchral resource that bears witness to the multicultural past of the Polish lands (see Table 10.1).

Religious cemeteries in Poland are mainly Roman Catholic cemeteries, which in canon law are called church cemeteries. They are distributed evenly throughout the country. According to Jacek Dziobek-Romański (1998), Roman Catholic cemeteries can be divided into:

• Parochial – as a rule intended for the burial of the dead of the faithful belonging to a particular parish, and owned by that parish.
• Interparish – a common cemetery intended for several parishes; such a situation occurs in practice mainly in larger cities, and is owned by the diocese.
• Monastic – for the burial of the deceased members of religious institutes.
• Special – intended for the burial of the dead of a specific group of people; they include cemeteries of chapters, confraternities, and institutes established under diocesan law.

According to the Code of Canon Law (1983), wherever possible the Church should have its own cemeteries or at least quarters in secular cemeteries for the burial of the faithful departed, duly blessed. The aforementioned code prohibits the burial of the dead in churches, unless it is the Bishop of Rome, cardinals, or diocesan bishops, including retired bishops, who should be buried in their own church (Drembkowski 2018).

Among the most interesting Roman Catholic sites are the national necropolises in Warsaw (Powązkowski Cemetery), Poznań (Cemetery of Merit), Sandomierz (St Joseph's Cemetery), Rzeszów (Old Cemetery), and Katowice Bogucice (Parish Cemetery). At the same time, it is the Powązki Cemetery that has been included (as the only site from Poland) in the list of 199 cemeteries in the world that must be seen before you die

Figure 10.2 Roman Catholic cemetery in Wasilków and monumental sculptures by Father Rabczyński built during the dark communist years. Photograph by Anna Długozima.

(Rhoads 2017). A cemetery unique to Poland is the site in Wasilków (see Figure 10.2). It contains seven groups of original cemetery sculptures relating to the Passion and Resurrection of Christ.

Jewish cemeteries are mainly located in the eastern, central, and southern parts of Poland. But as Samanta Kowalska stated (2012, 98), "in the interwar period, almost every bigger town in Poland had some kind of a structure for Jewish religious cult." The name most commonly used for a Jewish cemetery in Poland is *kirkut* (sometimes *kierkow* or *kierchol*). The Act on the relationship of the State to Jewish religious communities in the Republic of Poland (1997) guarantees the permanence of Jewish cemeteries (Drembkowski 2018). Facilities owned by Jewish communities or the Union of Jewish Religious Communities in Poland are not subject to expropriation (they are perpetual). Cemeteries owned by the State Treasury or local government units in relation to which regulatory proceedings have been initiated are subject to protection consisting, in particular, of a prohibition on their disposal to third parties and a prohibition on their use for other purposes. There is the Rabbinical Commission for Jewish Cemeteries within the Union of Jewish Communities in Poland. The Commission is a consultative and advisory body, and its task is to supervise Jewish cemeteries and the graves of Jews buried in other places. The guidelines of the Rabbinical Commission for Cemeteries on the protection of Jewish cemeteries in Poland form the key document defining the rules for cemetery work.

According to Bielawski's (2017) research, there are 1,164 Jewish cemeteries in Poland. Their condition varies substantially. Burials are

Figure 10.3 Jewish cemetery in Lesko. Photograph by Anna Długozima.

performed at seven cemeteries only, and these are in Bielsko, Katowice, Kraków, Legnica, Łódź, Warsaw, and Wrocław. In Żary, Szczecin and Poznań Jewish sections were demarcated at municipal cemeteries. In Poland is one of the oldest and most important Jewish cemeteries in Europe – the Remuh cemetery in Kraków. The largest Jewish cemetery in Europe, with the most impressive Jewish tombstones in the world, is the new Jewish cemetery in Łódź at Bracka Street. And the largest Jewish cemetery in Europe in terms of the number of tombstones is the cemetery in Warsaw at Okopowa Street (Olej-Kobus et al. 2009). However, other interesting Jewish cemeteries are in Lesko (see Figure 10.3), Lutowiska, Szczebrzeszyn, Szczepice, Mszczonów, Łowicz, and Szydłowiec.

Evangelical cemeteries are mainly located in the west, north, and southwestern parts of Poland. Two types of cemeteries can be observed, according to Anna E. Kubiak's (2018) typology: civilized necropolises (relatives of the dead look after the graves) and the forgotten and unwanted ones (abandoned necropolises), where natural succession usually takes place, and the graves are destroyed by nature itself (Puzdrakiewicz 2020). The first type includes active, historic cemeteries located in urban landscapes with well-preserved sepulchral substance; e.g., the Evangelical-Augsburg and the Evangelical-Reformed cemetery in Warsaw, in the Wola district. The Evangelical-Augsburg Cemetery was established in 1792. It was probably designed by the architect Szymon Bogumił Zug, and it contains many fine tombstones executed by the most outstanding sculptors. The oldest tombstones preserved in the churchyard are eclectic works drawn from Baroque art. These include many burial chapels; e.g., the monumental Halpert Chapel (1834), Skwarcov Chapel (1851), the mausoleum of the Braeunig family (1821), and the Dückert mausoleum (1828) (Skrodzka 2017). Well-known Evangelical cemeteries are located in Łódź (see Figure 10.4), with Karol Scheibler chapel – a masterpiece of neo-Gothic architecture, Bielsko-Biała, Lublin, and Wschowa as a unique monument to the funerary culture of the Lutheran bourgeoisie. The latter type comprises Evangelical cemeteries often located in forests, and they are not only gradually disappearing from the face of the Earth, but also from human awareness. Destroying Evangelical cemeteries was aimed at erasing the memory of the unwanted predecessors. The negative attitude to this heritage resulted from the time of occupation or forced resettlement to the Regained Territories. The Act on the relationship between the State and the Evangelical Lutheran Church in the Republic of Poland (1994) states in Article 28 that parishes have the right to own, manage, establish, and expand cemeteries (Drembkowski 2018).

Figure 10.4 The memorial of Sophie Biedermann is one of the most spectacular tombs in the Old Cemetery in Lodz (Evangelical section of the three-denominational necropolis). Photograph by Anna Długozima.

Figure 10.5 Cemetery around the Orthodox Church of the Dormition of the Mother of God in Wojnowo (Warmińsko-Mazurskie Voivodeship). Photograph by Anna Długozima.

Orthodox and Greek Catholic cemeteries are mainly located in the east and south of the country (the Carpathians). However, some of the largest ones are found in Warsaw, Sosnowiec, and Lublin. Particularly noteworthy are Lemko cemeteries in the Low Beskids (Bartne, Kotań), Boyko cemeteries in the Bieszczady Mountains (e.g. Berehy Górne, Wołosate, Bukowiec), Orthodox cemeteries on Mount Grabarka and the entire eastern region (e.g. Siemiatycze, Krynki). It is also worth remembering the Old Believers' cemeteries in Wojnowo (see Figure 10.5) and Gabowe Grądy (Stasiak, Tanaś 2005).

The Polish Autocephalous Orthodox Church has its legal status regulated by the Act on the relationship between the State and the Polish Autocephalous Orthodox Church (1991). In accordance with the above-mentioned regulations, the Orthodox Church is provided with the right to include investments in Orthodox cemeteries in the local spatial development plan. Allocation of land for the said purpose is made at the request of a diocesan bishop or a higher monastic superior (superior of a monastery). Orthodox cemeteries can be established not only on land owned by the Church but also on land owned by the State Treasury or local government units (Borecki 2007).

Cemeteries in Dubicze Cerkiewne have blue-painted gravestones. In Orthodoxy, blue symbolizes heaven, the mystery of existence, and is also the color of the Virgin Mary. Cemetery crosses are shaped like clovers. It is common practice to tie them with so-called embroideries. These are ribbons or pieces of fabric, hanging from the crosses as decoration and as a symbol of remembrance (Olej-Kobus et al. 2009).

Muslim cemeteries owned by the Muslim Religious Union in the Republic of Poland or by individual religious communes are subject to state regulations on religious cemeteries with regard to their establishment, expansion, closure, and management (Drembkowski 2018). Muslim cemeteries are called *mizars* by Polish Muslims. Currently, there are three active mizars in Poland, which are managed by the Muslim Religious Union in the Republic of Poland, in the Bohoniki (see Figure 10.6), Kruszyniany, and Warsaw. There are also historic mizars with an excluded burial function in Lebiedziewo and Studzianka. In addition, there are separate plots in the municipal cemeteries in Gdańsk, Trzcianka, Wrocław, Poznań, and Rybocice near Słubice (Drozd et al. 1999). A detailed description of all Muslim cemeteries existing in Poland is covered in the work of Andrzej Drozd et al. (1999).

It is also worth mentioning the Karaim Religious Union in the Republic of Poland, which has its legal status regulated by the Act on the relation of the State to the Karaim Religious Union in the Republic of Poland (1936). The Karaite cemetery is called a *zieriat*. This community's only cemetery in Poland is in Warsaw, at 34 Redutowa Street, established in 1890.

Figure 10.6 Mizar in the village Bohoniki (Podlaskie Voivodeship) with the status of a monument of history. Photograph by Anna Długozima.

War Cemeteries

The Act on War Graves and Cemeteries (1933) defines war cemeteries as cemeteries for the burial of the bodies of those killed fighting for the independence and the unity of the Polish State; military who were killed or who died because of the war, regardless of nationality; Sisters of Charity and all those doing the tasks assigned to them at any military formation who were killed or who died because of the war; prisoners of war and internees; refugees in 1915; military and civilian, regardless of their nationality, who lost their lives on account of the repression of the German or Soviet occupying forces after September 1, 1939; victims of German and Soviet camps who lost their lives on account of fighting against, or repression by, the imposed totalitarian system in the period from 1944 to 1956.

According to the legal regulations in force in Poland, the costs of construction and maintenance, including repairs of graves and cemeteries are charged to the state budget. Direct supervision over the condition of war graves and cemeteries is exercised by communities and municipalities. If communes do not have funds for this purpose, the funds should be allocated by a government administration body; i.e., the provincial governor.

War cemeteries are mainly connected with the period of WWI and WWII. According to a 1996 study commissioned by the Ministry of Spatial Planning and Construction, there were 1,574 sites in the territory of Poland relating to the events of WWI, including 974 independent cemeteries, 312 plots, and 288 mass graves. Graves and cemeteries of the WWII dead in Poland include more than 7,000 sites, with 333 independent cemeteries, 379 plots located in cemeteries, and about 6,300 mass and individual graves, located within cemeteries and outside cemeteries. In the Polish lands, the WWI cemeteries are grouped mainly along the front line of 1915, from Olsztyn to Kraków. Artistic, historical, and landscape values are represented by a unique complex of Western Galician war cemeteries, located on the territory of the Małopolskie Voivodeship and a part of the Podkarpackie Voivodeship. Their unique character is highlighted, among others, by the award of the European Heritage Label to cemetery No. 123 – Łużna-Pustki. WWII cemeteries are located practically on the entire territory of Poland. The most interesting, and most monumental of them are located in Warsaw (Powązki Wojskowe), Stare Łysogórki, and Palmiry.

Grave Arrangement

In Polish cemeteries, several standard solutions for the arrangement of grave fields can be identified, all of which are the results of two basic ways of orienting gravestones in relation to the sky and the ground:

vertical and horizontal. Detailed typology and characterization of gravestones can be found in Anna Sylwia Czyż and Bartłomiej Gutowski manual (2020).

Grave sites arranged with a vertical tombstone in the form of a cross, an obelisk, a column, or a statue prevailed until the interwar period. Nowadays, horizontal solutions dominate. Typical tombstone arrangements observed in the Polish cemeteries are:

1 A full grave memorial (the simplest type of tombstone); is placed over the whole of a grave and generally consists of kerbing surrounds, with a full granite cover (slab) to cover the middle of the grave, cement top, and stones or a garden bed.
2 A concrete, terrazzo, or granite headstone with grave surrounds (frame for a garden bed, artificial grass, or stones); decking wood frames are also available for graves.
3 A terrazzo or granite grave slab with a headstone (often in the form of a double grave).
4 A simple burial ground with a monument placed at the head of a grave.

Full grave memorials are decorated with cut flowers placed in vases or cuttings of garden plants such as begonias, or velvets placed in pots – which are an integral part of the grave arrangement. Plastic floral compositions and grave candles also appear (see Figure 10.7). The grave arrangement must be in accordance with the cemetery regulations. As Polish cemeteries are lacking in park infrastructure, grave

Figure 10.7 The most popular way of arranging a grave site in Poland, at a municipal cemetery in Szczęsne (Mazowieckie Voivodeship). Photograph by Anna Długozima.

Figure 10.8 Graveside bench with religious emblem and tool locker, a municipal
cemetery in Lidzbark Warmiński (Warmińsko-Mazurskie
Voivodeship). Photograph by Anna Długozima.

owners place benches in the grave field on their own, with the consent
of the cemetery manager. Currently, two models of grave-side benches
prevail in Poland: a folding one (see Figure 10.9) or one with a toolbox
(see Figure 10.8).

Due to the increasing popularity of cremation, cemetery managers
popularize American graves as an arrangement style (see Figure 10.10).

Kazimierz Mórawski (1989) notes that the era of individualized
sepulchral art ended as we entered the 20th century, especially with the
end of WWII. Since the middle of the 20th century, a mass pattern of
gravestones, unified for the whole country, has been observed in Poland
(with the disappearance of cultural and regional distinctions). However,
one can notice some differences conditioned by history and neighborhood. For example, in Silesia and Lower Silesia, due to rich mineral
resources, the families of the deceased opt mostly for natural stone when
choosing a grave setting. Stele gravestone monuments are popular in
cemeteries there. The vertical form of the tombstone creates space for
additional equipment or design elements. The popularity of this form of
gravestone should be linked to Poland's proximity to Germany (in terms
of the flow of ideas and patterns).

Figure 10.9 Simple burial ground with decking-wood frame and folding bench in a municipal cemetery in Koszalin (Zachodniopomorskie Voivodeship). Photograph by Anna Długozima.

Figure 10.10 Model of urn grave arrangement in a new municipal cemetery in Częstochowa (Śląskie Voivodeship). Photograph by Anna Długozima.

'Monumental Mason' Industry

"The Funeral Industry in Poland. Diagnosis and challenges" (Kolek et al. 2019) notes that there are 6,100 stonemasonry businesses in Poland. The Polish Stonemasonry Association (https://zpbk.pl/) was established on the initiative of employers to integrate the Polish environment related to the use of natural stone. The association has developed industry guidelines outlining the requirements for the production and erection of natural stone tombstones (PZK, 2019). This association was founded to support local stonemasonry in the face of the massive flooding of the market by tombstones from China. Cemeteries, regardless of their provenance, are beginning to look almost identical in every region of Poland. As Anna Królikowska stated (2012), contemporary Polish cemeteries are characterized by popular culture aesthetics.

Nowadays, tombstones are in most cases made by craftsmen and mass-produced. In opposition to this kitschy mass production of terrazzo and Chinese granite tombstones, studios specializing in designing original, minimalist sepulchral art are beginning to open up in Poland. They operate mainly in or near large cities. Art of Stone, Purest, and Granit Design are studios that exemplify a synergy of craftsmanship, design, and innovative solutions. In 2009, the Warsaw City Hall, together with the Office of the Capital Conservator of Monuments and the Warsaw branch of the Association of Polish Architects (SARP), announced a competition for the design of a contemporary tombstone recommended for historic cemeteries. The theme was a traditional grave plot in the context of the landscape of a historic cemetery. Although an important and necessary initiative, in the context of protecting the identity of historic cemeteries, it received little public attention.

References

Act on the Guarantees of the Freedom of Conscience and Faith, JoL 1989, No. 29, item. 155.

Act on the relation of the State to the Karaim Religious Union in the Republic of Poland, JoL 1936, No. 30, item. 241.

Act on the relationship between the State and the Evangelical Lutheran Church in the Republic of Poland, JoL 1994, No. 73, item. 323.

Act on the relationship between the State and the Polish Autocephalous Orthodox Church, JoL 1991, No. 66, item. 287.

Act on the relationship of the State to Jewish religious communities in the Republic of Poland, JoL 1997, No. 41, item. 251.

Act on war graves and cemeteries, JoL 1933, No. 39, item. 311.

Bielawski Krzysztof 2017, "Ohele w Polsce z uwzględnieniem ich występowania na cmentarzach wielkomiejskich" (Ohels in Poland with consideration of their occurrence in metropolitan cemeteries) (in:) Gadowska I. (ed.), *Wielkomiejskie cmentarze żydowskie w Europie Środkowo-Wschodniej* (Urban Jewish cemeteries in Central and Eastern Europe), Łódź. http://cmentarze-zydowskie.pl/ohele_w_polsce.pdf [10.04.2022].

Borecki Paweł, 2007, "Zasada równouprawnienia wyznań w prawie polskim" (The principle of equal rights of religions in Polish law), Studia z Prawa Wyznaniowego, 10, 115–159.

Code of Canon Law. https://www.katolicki.net/ftp/kodeks_prawa_kanonicznego.pdf [21.04.2022].

98   *Anna Długozima*

Czyż Sylwia Anna, Gutowski Bartłomiej 2020, *Podręcznik do inwentaryzacji polskich cmentarzy i nagrobków poza granicami kraju* (Manual for the inventory of Polish cemeteries and gravestones abroad), Polonika, Warszawa.

Długozima Anna 2020, "Social infrastructure of burial nature in Poland by voivodships – conditions and directions of changes", *Acta Scientiarum Polonorum Administratio Locorum*, 19(1), 19–31.

Długozima Anna 2022, "How to find a suitable location for a cemetery? Application of multi-criteria evaluation for identifying potential sites for cemeteries in Białystok, Poland", *Moravian Geographical Reports*, 30(1), 34–53.

Drembkowski Paweł 2018, *Ustawa o cmentarzach i chowaniu zmarłych. Komentarz* (Law on Cemeteries and Burial of the Dead. Commentary), Wydawnictwo C.H. Beck, Warszawa.

Drozd Andrzej, Dziekan Marek M., Majda Tadeusz 1999, *Meczety i cmentarze Tatarów polsko-litewskich* (Mosques and cemeteries of the Polish-Lithuanian Tatars), Res Publica Multiethnica, Warszawa.

Dziobek-Romański Jacek 1998, "Cmentarze – zarys regulacji historycznych, prawnych i kanonicznych" (Cemeteries – an outline of historical, legal and canonical regulations), *Rocznik Historyczno – Archiwalny*, T. XIII, Przemyśl, 3–32.

Kolek Antoni, Lang Grzegorz, Kozłowski Łukasz 2019, *Branża pogrzebowa w Polsce. Diagnoza i wyzwania* (The funeral industry in Poland. Diagnosis and challenges), CALPE sp. z o.o., Warszawa.

Królikowska Anna 2012, Estetyka współczesnych cmentarzy (Aesthetics of contemporary cemeteries), *Opuscula Sociologica*, No. 1, 59–72.

Kubiak Anna E. 2018, "Civilized and wild heterotopia – the case of the Polish cemeteries", *Anthropological Researches and Studies*, 8, 276–284.

Michałowski Andrzej 1995, "Ochrona cmentarzy w Polsce" (Cemetery protection in Poland) (in:) Czerner O., Juszkiewicz I. (eds.), *Cemetery Art – Sztuka Cmentarna – l'art de cimetiere*, ICOMOS, Wrocław.

Mórawski Kazimierz 1989, *Przewodnik historyczny po cmentarzach warszawskich* (Historical guide to Warsaw cemeteries), Wydawnictwo PTTK "Kraj", Warszawa.

NID 2017, *Raport o stanie zachowania zabytków nieruchomych w Polsce. Zabytki wpisane do rejestru zabytków* (Report on the state of preservation of immovable monuments in Poland. Monuments in the register of monuments). https://nid.pl/wp-content/uploads/2021/11/RAPORT-O-STANIE-ZACHOWANIA-ZABYTKOW-NIERUCHOMYCH.pdf [10.03.2022].

NIK 2016, *Zarządzanie cmentarzami komunalnymi* (Management of municipal cemeteries). https://www.nik.gov.pl/plik/id,12230,vp,14613.pdf [10.04.2022].

Olej-Kobus Anna, Kobus Krzysztof, Rembas Michał 2009, *Nekropolie. Zabytkowe cmentarze wielokulturowej Polski* (Necropolies. Historic cemeteries of multicultural Poland), Carta Blanca, Warszawa.

Puzdrakiewicz Krystian, "Cemeteries as (un)wanted heritage of previous communities. An example of changes in the management of cemeteries and their social perception in Gdańsk, Poland", Landscape Online, 86, 1–26.

PZK 2019, Stone Masonry Industry Standards. http://www.zpbk.pl/download/wytycznenagrobki/wytyczne_1_01.pdf [10.04.2022].

Rhoads Loren 2017, *199 Cemeteries to See Before You Die*, London, Sphere.

Rogowska Barbara 2014, "Stanowisko władz komunistycznych w latach siedemdziesiątych XX wieku w zakresie cmentarnictwa wyznaniowego i komunalnego" (The position of the communist regime on the religious and communal cemeteries in the 1970s.), *Annales Universitatis Paedagogicae Cracoviensis. Studia Politologica XIII*, 165, 75–93.

Skrodzka Agnieszka 2017, "Nagrobki osobistości z końca XVIII i 1. połowy XIX stulecia na Cmentarzu Ewangelicko-Augsburskim w Warszawie" (Tombstones of important people in the Evangelical-Augsburg cemetery in Warsaw at the turn of the 19th century), *Rocznik Historii Sztuki*, XLII, 173–191.

Sobotka Sławomir, Długozima Anna 2015, Evaluation and development opportunities of the disused Lutheran cemeteries within the Maskulińskie and Pisz forest divisions for thanatourism, *Tourism*, 25/1, 67–75.

Stasiak Andrzej, Tanaś Sławoj 2005, "Przestrzeń sepulkralna w turystyce" (The sepulchral space in Tourism), *Turystyka i Hotelarstwo*, 8, 9–42.

Starzecka Katarzyna 2014, "Lokalizacja cmentarza wyznaniowego w świetle przepisów prawa polskiego o planowaniu i zagospodarowaniu przestrzennym" (Location of religious cemetery on the basis of the polish law provisions of the spatial planning and land use management), *Studia z Prawa Wyznaniowego*, 17, 173–191.

11   Cremation

Anna E. Kubiak and Anna Długozima

The Proportion of Deaths Followed by Cremation

Compared with its popularity in other European countries, cremation in Poland is not a prevalent form of disposing of remains. The factors contributing to the steadily low numbers of cremations in Poland compared with elsewhere in Europe include the association of cremation (especially for the early post-war generation) with the extermination camps of WWII; traditionalist pressure in smaller towns and in the countryside; and the influence of certain representatives of the Catholic clergy who are against cremation. The Catholic Church permits cremation as long as it is not done for reasons contrary to the Christian faith. However, it recommends a traditional funeral. Cremation burial was approved by the Polish bishops in a letter formulated at the plenary meeting of the Polish Bishops' Conference in Przemyśl, October 14–16, 2011. The letter expressed the church's position allowing cremation but recommending that the remains be buried, because – according to the bishops – in this way respect is given. In the letter, the bishops also expressed their opposition to the scattering of ashes, even in designated cemetery spaces.

Factors affecting the increase in cremations are the lower funeral price (although this depends on such factors as transport); the growing availability of crematoria; the promotion of cremation by business owners; the rising number of exhumations in order to bury the dead in one grave vis-à-vis the relatively easy addition of an urn to the family grave; and the decreasing space available in cemeteries.

New generations are changing their attitudes toward cremation, and it is most popular among young people from bigger cities, with higher education and working in managerial positions, and among white-collar workers. Women more often accept cremation, while farmers, retirees, and pensioners are the least likely to choose this option Gajewska (2009, 223). Lastly, the pandemic brought a sharp increase in the number of cremations.

DOI: 10.4324/9781003207634-11

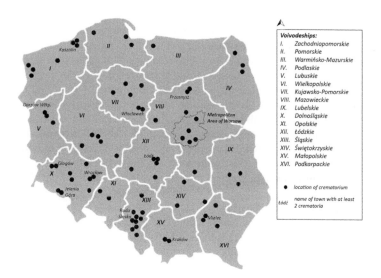

Figure 11.1 Spatial distribution of crematoria in Poland, taking into account location in relation to the cemetery. By Anna Długozima.

As of June 2022, there are 74 crematoria in Poland, of which 11 are municipal.[1] These crematoria are located primarily in the southwestern and central provinces (see Figure 11.1).

The Cremation Society of Great Britain has recognized Poland as one of the most dynamically developing markets in cremation services in Europe. In 2007 there were ten crematoria in Poland. After 2010, sudden growth in the number of crematoria was recorded: 20 in 2012; 51 in 2016; 53 in 2017; 54 in 2018; and 61 in 2019.

The number of cremations in Poland is difficult to precisely determine, due to the fact that no statistical data is collected on the number of cremations. The funeral industry is not obliged to disclose these statistics and the owners of crematories hide behind trade secrets for fear of competition. Due to the limited availability of data, I provide only an estimate of the proportion of deaths followed by cremation. In 2016, cremations accounted for approximately 24% of funerals in Poland (Kolek et al. 2019, 26). During the pandemic, although cremation was not mandated, funeral homes put pressure on customers to choose cremation. As a result, the number of cremations increased significantly, and in 2021 cremations comprised about 40% of funerals. In larger cities, they comprised about 60%.

Scenarios of Ceremonies Held in Crematoria

The Catholic Church recommends that rituals accompanying cremation consist of two parts: a mass with the coffin before cremation, and then placing the urn in the cemetery. This recommendation lengthens the whole rite of passage to two days or even longer and involves an increase in costs, especially because the modest cremation coffin – according to many – is not suitable for presenting on a catafalque in the church. However, the bishops allow for the possibility of a Mass with an urn when the ashes are brought from abroad and when relatives of the deceased have come from distant places and cannot participate in both phases of the ceremony. The family must ask the pastor for permission to have an urn Mass. In practice, this issue is left to the local parishes to decide.

Many factors are considered in setting the stage with the funeral home consultant, such as which crematory is to perform the service, whether the memorial service is to be held with a casket or with an urn, the participation of the family in the various phases of the rite of passage, the disposition of the ashes, and the vigil at the urn. In addition to the family, the possible choices are influenced by the crematorium and its offerings, and the local priest. The multitude of possible options means that there are several cremation funeral scenarios. The family chooses a cremation coffin and an urn. The Polish funeral market has a wide range of urns, and the material used to make them may be wood, stone, ceramic, marble, brass, or glass.

The final farewell, lasting from 15 minutes to half an hour, may take place before or after the service. If the cremation takes place in a different location from where the family lives, then the family often does not go to the cremation (possibly only one or two people) and the farewell ceremony takes place before the coffin is transported to the incinerator. Crematories have chapels in their buildings for this purpose; sometimes the farewell ceremony takes place in the chapel of the funeral home. The cremation coffin is usually made of pine or alder wood without varnish (or covered with a special eco-friendly one) and the relevant metal fittings. Sometimes a priest accompanies the family in the last farewell. Individual preferences are also permitted. It is possible to play one's own music, put up a photo, and display photos and videos of the deceased in the form of slides.

In the crematorium, the family can watch the coffin go into the oven if they wish. An employee pushes the coffin on a cart or on a carrier placed on rails toward a lock in the wall that separates this room from the invisible technical room. Depending on the crematorium, the family watches the process by looking through the glass in the room next door, or a room on another floor of the building is made available and the family watches the operation on a monitor. The strictly technical part takes place in a room with a furnace, which is never accessible to the family during the funeral. In the farewell room, the family only sees the coffin enter an open airlock in the wall, behind which the furnace is located. This is accompanied by music chosen by the relatives or suggested by the company. However, many families choose not to watch the coffin enter the oven. The moment is brief and is a traumatic experience for many mourners.

The cremation ovens are located in vaults inaccessible to mourners. Meanwhile, workers at the crematorium proceed to burn the body, which takes from one and a half to two hours. The ashes are given to the funeral company in an urn. Burial usually takes place the day after cremation. In some crematoria, the family can stay with the urn in the farewell room. So, we have another new practice: vigils with the ashes of the deceased. Mourners also have the option of taking the urn home for a day or two and taking it to the cemetery themselves or having a company do it for them. A memorial service with the urn may then take place. On the other hand, in some localities, if the priest does not agree, there may be a service without a coffin and without an urn.

The Disposition of Ashes

Multiple scenarios also arise in the phase of disposing of the ashes. According to Polish law, an urn must be buried in a cemetery. Here, too, various burial options arise, depending on the cemetery manager. It may be an urn wall called a columbarium, an urn post, an urn plot, or a family tomb. Sometimes the family buries the urn with the personal belongings of the deceased. The urn burial ceremony – itself impoverished – can be enhanced by the crematory. Some crematories provide a ceremonial setting for the funeral in the form of small pillows, or catafalques for the urn, along with other decorations that make the atmosphere of the ceremony more solemn.

At times, It happens – according to the estimates of company managers, about 5% of the time – that the family takes the urn and does not deliver it to the cemetery, or buries an empty urn. According to the will of the deceased, the ashes are then (illegally) scattered on the ground or in the sea. It also happens that urns are kept at home.

The last practice is to pour out part of the ashes into reliquaries purchased at a funeral home, to be placed at home, for example, with a framed photo of the deceased, but also in the form of pendants. The name refers to relics made of body parts (often fingers) of saints. We can associate this practice with the 18th- and 21st-century custom of keeping lockets of hair closed in pendants, medallions, or brooches (Ariès 1989, 379) (Figure 11.2).

Figure 11.2 Reliquaries sold at trade fairs in Poznań. Photograph by Anna E. Kubiak.

In Poland, the possibility of scattering ashes existed for a very short time. The law of 1959 did not regulate the fate of ashes. When "Memorial Gardens" were established in the 1990s, they gradually gained supporters. In 2006, the Ministry of Health prepared a provision to allow the scattering of ashes in Memorial Gardens, in an amendment to the Law on Cemeteries and Burial of the Dead. However, in the same year, the government withdrew from this version of the law. Memorial Gardens exist in Poznań, Ruda Śląska, Szczecin, and Warsaw. In Poland, in some of the 'Memorial Gardens' a ceremony is performed to bury the ashes rather than scattering them. In this way, the ban is circumvented. It is also possible to place a commemorative plaque with the person's details on a wall designated for this purpose. There are also companies in Poland that transmute a part of the ashes (about 200 grams) into diamonds – *diatanats* – which are then set in jewelry.

Crematoria Design

According to the Building Law Act (1994) and Polish Classification of Building Objects (1999), crematoria are included in class 1272: "Buildings intended for religious worship and religious activities ("Churches, chapels, Orthodox churches, mosques, synagogues, cemeteries and related facilities, funeral parlors, and crematoria"). Moreover, in the Polish Classification of Products and Services (2015), cremation is classified as a service activity in the category of funerals and related activities.

Crematoria are included in the program of necropolises designed in Poland today. Examples are the following municipal cemeteries with 21st-century provenance: Częstochowa (2003), Karakule (2010), Jaszków (2013), Nowa Chełmża (2014), and Podgórki Tynieckie (2020).

The increase in public interest in cremation meant that in the historical, already-formed layout of many cemeteries, a place for a crematorium had to be found. For example, at the Miłostowo cemetery in Poznań, Fort III was adapted for a crematorium. At the Central Cemetery in Szczecin and Municipal Cemetery Rzeszów-Wilkowyja, a crematorium was organized in the cemetery chapel, while in Antoninów and Bytom – in the building of the funeral parlor (Długozima 2020). To summarize, in the functional and spatial structure of the Polish cemetery, the crematorium is:

A Located in a multifunctional facility, in which, apart from the incineration plant, there are rooms dedicated to administrative and funeral services (florist, dissecting room, funeral parlor); e.g., Antoninów, Częstochowa, Nowa Chełmża, Ruda Śląska "Memorial Park", Warsaw.

B An independent architectural object (in a cemetery space, many buildings are dedicated to funeral functions); e.g., Jaszków, Dąbrowa Górnicza, Wrocław – Psie Pole.

Although contemporary architecture is accompanied by a process called *typological uniformization* by Andrzej Jasiński (2012), an analysis of the spatial forms of contemporary crematoria in Poland indicates a certain diversity. There are three dominant trends in crematorium architecture, referring to residential architecture, service and production architecture, and religious architecture (see Table 11.1). References to the above-mentioned types of construction result from current legislation and the perception of crematoria in Polish society (Długozima 2020). Reminiscences of residential architecture are due to the fact that in many cases crematorium complements the funeral home program. A crematorium has to meet the conditions of the technological process and the environmental requirements, which is why its convergence with industrial architecture is emphasized in the design.

A common feature of Polish crematoria is the color of the facades, resulting from universal preferences for earth colors and nature. The colors used are dominated by brown and rust (using corten steel, brick, and clinker; e.g., crematoria in Ramlewo, Bytom, Częstochowa, Jaszków, Poznań, Ruda Śląska, Szczecin). This range of colors is associated with symbolism, as these shades indicate transience, the relationship of man with the earth ("you are dust and to dust you shall

Table 11.1 References to residential, services, and religious architecture in the design of contemporary crematoria. Own elaboration based on Długozima (2020)

Trends in crematorium architecture referring to …	Features	Examples
Residential Architecture	Stylistics of the Polish court; gable, pediment, and mansard roofs	Kalisz; Otwock; Wyszków; Pruszków (see Figure 11.3); Przasnysz
Service and Production Architecture	No emblems; simple, modern form; concrete, glass (large transparent surfaces), corten	Karakule (see Figure 11.4); Katowice; Lubin; Nowa Chełmża; Ramlewo; Strzelin; Stalowa Wola; Toruń; Włocławek
Religious Architecture	Presence of elements associated with sacred buildings, i.e. tower, portico, arcade, belfry, dome, religious emblems (identification of archetypal sacred elements)	Antoninów (see Figure 11.5); Bytom; Częstochowa; Gorzów Wlkp. "Dom Pogrzebowy"; Łódź; Słupsk; Wrocław; Szczecin

Figure 11.3 Architecture of a crematorium in Pruszków (Mazowieckie Voivodeship) is reminiscent of residential architecture. Photograph by Anna Długozima.

Figure 11.4 Architecture of a crematorium in Karakule (Podlaskie Voivodeship) is reminiscent of services architecture. Photograph by Anna Długozima.

return"). Because concrete is a common material today, shades of gray (e.g., Antoninów, Białe Błota, Białystok, Dąbrowa Górnicza, Garbce, Nowa Chełmża) are also used in crematoria facades. There are also several objects with black facades: granite (e.g., Opole), clinker (e.g., Toruń), and panels with fiber cement structures (e.g., Głogów, Radom).

The design approach, dominating in Poland in the context of crematoria, represents the modernist architecture featured by universal forms, with no signs of locality. The building is neither a church, nor a

Figure 11.5 View on the main square with the entrance to the crematorium and
administration buildings in Antoninów (Mazowieckie Voivodeship).
Photograph by Anna Długozima.

chapel, nor a house, but a sober and righteous object. Devoid of any
symbolic ornamentation, the crematorium and its surroundings are to be
used by people of all faiths (ecumenical character of the building).
Minimalism is also a way of camouflaging the architecture of death. Jan
Zamasz (2007, 192) concluded that the "element of sacrum is hidden by
a far-reaching metaphor. This attitude arises from the aesthetics, the
source of which is the Protestant religion". In Antoninów, the crematorium and other facilities associated with the funeral ceremony (chapel,
waiting room, entrance hall) was hidden inside an artificial hill – a
Slavic burial mound – symbolizing a gateway to another, better world.
Moreover, two chapels (ceremonial halls) have been designed, one with
religious decor and the other secular. The building is full of clear symbols
related to death and funerals.

   In Polish designs, the convention for masking crematorium chimneys
is observed. It is developing by introducing columns and panels in the
façade of buildings that are the architectural equivalent of trees (e.g.,
crematorium in Białe Błota, Karakule, Radom).

   Moreover, references to the architecture of European crematoria
in Polish projects can be found. For example, the porticos of the

crematoria in Antoninów, Karakule, and Radom were echoed by the portico of Gunnar Asplund's Woodland Crematorium, picturesquely situated at the Skogskyrkogarden cemetery.

Notes

1 I cite the website administered by Krzysztof Wolicki, president of the Polish Funeral Association: "Krematoria w Polsce" (Crematoria in Poland). Krematoria w Polsce / Lewe menu - PHU Krzysztof [10.02.2022]. Poland also has seven crematoria for animals.

References

Ariès Philippe 1989, *Człowiek i śmierć* (The hour of our death), PIW, Warszawa.

Building Law Act, JoL 1994, No.89, item. 414.

Długozima Anna 2020, "How might landscapes be better designed to accommodate increasing cremation practices in Europe?", *Landscape Online*, vol. 87, 1–31.

Gajewska Magdalena 2009, *Prochy i Diamenty. Kremacja ciała zmarłego człowieka jako zjawisko społeczne i kulturowe* (Ashes and Diamonds. Cremation of the body of a dead person as a social and cultural phenomenon), Nomos, Kraków.

Jasiński Andrzej 2012, "O zjawisku dematerializacji formy architektury współczesnej" (On dematerialization of forms of contemporary architecture), *Czasopismo Techniczne. Architektura*, vol. 5-A/2, 240–245.

Kolek Antoni, Lang Grzegorz, Kozłowski Łukasz 2019, *Branża pogrzebowa w Polsce* (The funeral industry in Poland), Centrum Analiz Legislacyjnych i Polityki Ekonomicznej, Warszawa.

Polish Classification of Building Facilities, JoL 1999, No. 112, item. 1316.

Polish Classification of Products and Services, JoL 2015, item. 1676.

Zamasz Jan 2007, "Architektura cmentarza komunalnego w Świdniku k. Lublina. Autorskie doświadczenie projektowo-realizacyjne" (Architecture of the municipal cemetery in Swidnik by Lublin. Project and constructing experience of the author), *Teka Komisji Arch.-Urb. i Studiów Krajobrazowych*, vol. 3, 189–202.

12 Commemoration and Memoralisation

Anna Długozima and
Agnieszka Wedeł-Domaradzka

All Souls' Day and Visits to the Graves

All Saints Day, falling on the 1st of November is an official public holiday in Poland. Some parishes celebrate holy masses in the cemeteries and solemn processions combined with prayer for the dead. This celebration continues through to All Souls' Day, which is on the 2nd of November but is not an official (public) holiday. The 2nd of November is known as *Dzień Zaduszny, Zaduszki*, or *Święto Zmarłych* in Polish (Commemoration of All the Faithful Departed and the Day of the Dead).

The Polish background of All Souls' Day comes from an ancient Slavic feast called *Dziady*, which means Forefathers. It was universally believed that on the night of the 1st of November to the 2nd, after nightfall the souls of the dead came down to earth and made their way to their former homes and, at midnight, to the church, where a dead priest held mass (Kubica 1986, Ogrodowska 2007). The ritual of visiting graves in the first two days of November has been practised in Poland since the 19th century. As Kubica (1986) noted, the symbol of fire and flowers appear in the All Souls' Day ceremony. Fire has always been of fundamental significance in folk culture. Good souls are said to enter a world of light and wicked souls a world of darkness. Cemeteries are particularly spectacular on the 1st and 2nd of November after dark, when they glow with thousands of candles (called *znicze* in Polish) and lanterns.

From the postwar period (especially from the Polish People's Republic), the plant symbol of the 1st and 2nd of November celebrations is the chrysanthemum. Introduced from the Far East, it has been recognised as an ideal plant for grave decorations due to its resistance to frost and late flowering time (Polish autumn) (Jabłońska, Sobczak 2011). This is a family festival to which relatives often come from considerable distances. On All Saints' Day and All Souls' Day, the annual campaign *Snitch (Znicz)* is organised by the police, and consists of patrols of roads, traffic control in the vicinity of cemeteries, and sobriety controls.

DOI: 10.4324/9781003207634-12

A few days beforehand, someone from the family tidies up the graves of the relatives and plants flowers on them (see Figures 12.1 and 12.2). Religious Poles mark this day by going to church and bringing *wypominki*, a list of deceased family members and friends to be read from the altar during Mass. In the vicinity of the cemeteries, temporary stalls

Figure 12.1 The graves of former residents of the Świątki village are cleaned and decorated with chrysanthemums in the church cemetery (Warmińsko-Mazurskie Voivodeship). Photograph by Anna Długozima.

Figure 12.2 Cleaning of the graves by the Glotowo inhabitants one week before the 1st and 2nd of November celebrations (Warmińsko-Mazurskie Voivodeship). Photograph by Anna Długozima.

with flowers, decorations, grave candles, and cemetery accessories are organised. In many places in Poland, for the 1st and 2nd of November, the surroundings of the cemeteries change – they acquire a fair and ludic character. There are toy vendors, most of them with balloons, and food vendors offering candyfloss, ice cream, and bagels. Moreover, traditional sweet titbits still can be bought, and include ladies' crust (*pańska skórka* in Polish), Turkish honey (*miodek turecki*), and sliver (*szczypka*) (Landowski 2000, Tanaś 2020).

Some parishes and non-governmental organisations have organised collections for the rescue of historic monuments at Polish cemeteries.

It should be emphasised that Poles visit graves not only on 1 and 2 November, but, according to surveys conducted systematically by CBOS (from 1998 to 2020), also during the celebration of Christmas, and Easter. In the most recent survey (in 2020), 83% of respondents declared that they visit the graves on the anniversaries of their relatives' deaths on these days. They always leave an empty chair and plate at the table, as if waiting for those who were gone and so that no one is scared about their arrival. Moreover, before Christmas, they decorate graves with fir spruce branches, and before Easter, the graves are decorated with flowers or catkins. Poles also celebrate the anniversaries of their relatives' deaths. A memorial Mass is celebrated on the first anniversary of a loved one's death. In some families, each subsequent anniversary is marked in this manner. In others, the commemoration is limited to the first anniversary and later to 'round' ones (5th, 10th, etc.). After the anniversary mass, family and relatives visit the grave, lay flowers, and light candles.

It is also a practice in Poland to visit the graves of parents and grandparents on the day of a family wedding.

Decoration and Maintaining the Grave

A common tradition across Poland is to own a plot at a cemetery in advance (either for oneself or the whole family) (Pietkiewicz 2012).

In Poland, companies have recently formed to professionally clean graves. The service can be provided as a one-off task or can be cyclical (subscription), or on an occasional basis, and includes cleaning, washing, and care of the area around the grave. The offer is addressed primarily to people living abroad, seniors, and those who, due to health reasons, are unable to personally maintain the graves of their relatives' deaths. In the database of information about Polish funeral companies, one can find a list of entities whose activities are profiled in the area of grave care (e.g., https://funer.com.pl). Regionalisation is noticeable – cleaning companies operate mainly in large cities and their vicinity.

The anniversary of a death is often also the time when Poles enrich the burial site with new grave decorations. There is an informal tradition that a headstone unveiling should take place within a year of the death.

Wreaths and bouquets are mainly used to decorate graves. Wreaths in Poland are usually made on a base of tree branches and coniferous bushes. When decorating graves, Poles give priority to the durability of the composition (desirable properties of plants are frost resistance, ease of care, drought resistance), hence the popularity of potted plants (velvet, coleus, royal begonia, chrysanthemum, shrub gilt) and ground-planted chrysanthemums, heathers, common heather, bulbous plants (lilies, calla lilies), evergreens and coniferous plants (periwinkle, boxwood).

Memorials in Public Spaces

Memorials are places related to the struggle for independence, wars or repression, combat or martyrdom, and monuments, memorial plaques, and other objects and signs commemorating soldiers and civilian victims of war. The issue of memorials is not regulated in Polish law by a separate legal act. However, the sites of remembrance are mentioned in international agreements concluded by Poland concerning cooperation with other countries with regard to taking care of graves and, more precisely, sites of remembrance.

The international agreements include obligations to register graves and memorials, exchange information on their location, maintain memorials and cemeteries, support their decoration and commemoration, and provide an appropriate environment befitting the solemnity of such places. In addition, within the framework of mutual obligations, there are also those concerning the importation of equipment, means, and materials necessary for establishing these places, as well as ensuring free access to the citizens of the other state to memorials and resting places.

The protection of memorials is based on the regulations on museums and the protection of monuments. In addition to monuments commonly understood as material creations commemorating persons or events, mounds, obelisks, columns, sculptures, statues, busts, memorial stones, plaques, and commemorative plaques located on real estate owned or held by a local authority, an association of local authorities or a metropolitan association are also considered monuments (Article 2, paragraph 4, Act of 24 February 2022).

A separate category of memorials in public spaces is a form of commemoration placed at the site of a death. These are earliest represented by roadside crosses erected at the site of road accidents. However, other forms of commemoration also occur; e.g., bicycles in the case of cyclists' deaths or toys in the case of children's deaths (Przybylska 2022). Small memorials are less common. These sites are overwhelmingly maintained and visited by relatives, as expressed, for example, by burning candles. From a legal perspective, this form of commemoration is not regulated. However, the problem may be the location of these forms of commemoration – close to roads, for example – which may lead to their removal in the absence of permission from the road manager.

The Monument of "Crossing" in Zabawa near Tarnów was erected in 2010–2012 as a response to the need to establish a space of contemplation and meeting for people injured in road traffic accidents and their families, as well as a place to commemorate those killed. Every year the illumination of a symbolic light, the planting of a tree of memory, meetings with the families of the victims, therapeutic workshops, educational programs, scientific seminars, and conferences are held at the monument.

War and Holocaust Commemoration

Unique legal solutions were enacted for places related to the need to commemorate the war and the Holocaust.

According to the Law of 1933, war graves are the graves and resting places of the fallen in the struggle for the independence and unification of the Polish State, military persons killed or deceased due to warfare, regardless of nationality, Sisters of Mercy, and all persons who died while on duty at any military formation, or died due to warfare, as well as prisoners of war and internees, refugees from 1915, military and civilian persons, regardless of their nationality, who lost their lives as a result of repression by the German or Soviet occupying forces from 1 September 1939, victims of German and Soviet camps, including cemeteries for their ashes, persons who lost their lives as a result of fighting against the imposed totalitarian system or as a result of totalitarian repression or ethnic cleansing from 8 November 1917 to 31 July 1990. The law introduces the obligation to care for war graves and surround them with due respect and solemnity regardless of the nationality and religion of the persons buried in them and the formations to which they belonged (Article 2, Law of 28 March 1933).

Funds necessary for constructing and maintaining war graves and cemeteries come from the state budget. These tasks may be entrusted, by agreement, to a local self-government unit, which also equips itself with appropriate funds, or they may be performed by foundations, associations, and social institutions, which are entitled to apply for an appropriate subsidy. Legal solutions for the commemoration of the Holocaust are contained in the Act concerning the Martyrdom of the Polish Nation and other Peoples at Auschwitz (Act of 2 July 1947) and the Act on the Protection of the Areas of the Former Nazi Death Camps (Act of 7 May 1999). The first of these legal acts designated the grounds of the Auschwitz camp, together with all the buildings and facilities therein, as a Monument to the Martyrdom of the Polish Nation and Other Peoples, while also indicating that a museum is to be created on the grounds. The second piece of legislation sets out the rules for the protection of the sites of former Nazi extermination camps. The protection envisaged by the law consists of the creation of their protection zones as well as the introduction of special rules in the area of the Holocaust Memorials and their protection zones concerning the holding of assemblies, the conduct of economic activities, the construction of buildings, temporary buildings and construction equipment, and the expropriation of real estate.

Virtual Commemoration

Virtual Cemetery[1] is a web-based system that resembles a simulation game (Bykowski, Bober 2015). Similar to the above-mentioned website is The Gardens of Memories ("Ogród Wspomnień"[2]), founded in 2007. Nekropolis[3] is an IT system for cemetery managers (the so-called Interactive Cemetery Administrator), which combines an interactive map with a database of the graves and buried persons. It is the most frequently chosen cemetery management software in Poland because it supports the work of the cemetery administration in all the necessary scopes. Due to this, it is aimed more at the institutional user rather than the individual user. GroboNet[4] is an application that enables users to find the burial place of a deceased person from a web browser. WebCmentarz[5] is a system that stores the data of grave keepers and photographs of gravestones. Mogiły[6] is a nationwide cemetery search engine with burial indexes. Moreover, the Cultural Heritage Foundation has launched a mobile app, Cmentariusz, that allows people to document abandoned cemeteries they encounter in order to build a database of forgotten burial grounds in Poland and the wider region. On the internet, one can also find the so-called Polish funeral platforms, which aggregate data of companies operating in the funeral industry.[7]

Pro-Ecological Practices

The Polish traditional forms of burial, graves, tombstones, and commemoration practices are harmful to the environment. Tons of concrete, hardwood (oak), metals (coffin hardware, headstone components) are used to build graves (formerly earthen). Artificial flowers, candles, and reeds brought to the graves later become waste. According to some estimates, piles of garbage in cemeteries, especially after All Saints' Day, amount to as much as a city of 100,000 people produces each year (more than 30 tons). According to calculations by the Communal Portal,[8] Poles buy around 300 million candles every year: eight per person. Therefore, acting to reduce the production of rubbish should undoubtedly be considered a step towards environmental protection in Poland.

As environmental awareness is growing in Poland, so is interest in ecological burials. More and more Polish cemeteries and funeral directors are trying to be environmentally friendly by implementing pro-ecological solutions, in terms of cemetery management (Długozima, Kosiacka-Beck 2020), funerary accessories, and promoted practices.

In cemetery architecture, it has been observed that using creeping plants on building facades (green walls) (see Figure 12.3) and planting gardens on their roofs (see Figure 12.4) are solutions that lead to the reduction of heating or cooling energy in the building, increasing biodiversity and biological active areas. Solar energy and LED lighting are more popular in reducing costs of maintenance and heat emissions, and also increasing social awareness. More popular in cemetery development is using a diversity of plants and mineral surfaces in transportation systems.

In order to reduce the impact of Polish commemorative culture on the environment, ecological practices such as *Zniczodzielnia* ("recycling rack for candles"), "Without artificiality" (buying natural flowers), "Self-made and creative" (self-made grave decorations), "Be eco at the

Figure 12.3 Climbers covering a ceremonial building, municipal cemetery in Czestochowa. Photograph by Anna Długozima.

Figure 12.4 A green roof of a building complex that is completely covered with vegetation. Southern Municipal Cemetery in Antoninów. Photograph by Anna Długozima.

cemetery!" (segregating cemetery waste) are becoming increasingly popular in Poland. Eco-friendly funeral products on the Polish funeral market include wicker coffins and urns, manufactured so far mainly for export to England, Germany, Sweden, and Denmark (e.g. MR Wiklina, Eco-Hades, Wiklinopol, Peewit), and cremation coffins made of FSC-certified wood or paperboard for low-cost traditional burials and cremations. Eco-friendly products manufactured in Poland are also the "Kami" biodegradable urn (created by NURN – a brand which specialising in premium urn design and production), biodegradable candle ground (designed by Klaudia Ginter) and the "Ovo" biodegradable urn (designed by Małgorzata Dziembaj). In part of the municipal cemetery near Poznan a "Forest of Remembrance" has been established – a place where the dead will be laid to rest in biodegradable urns. There will be no tombstones, crosses, flowers, or candles. It is a specially designated place to be used for the ecological burial of the dead. The new "Law on cemeteries and funerals" prepared in 2021 by the Community Initiative "(Un)forgotten cemeteries" assumes the possibility of green burials and cemeteries.

Notes

1 https://wirtualnycmentarz.pl/, https://virtualgrave.eu/.
2 In Polish, www.ogrodywspomnien.pl.
3 https://polskie-cmentarze.com/.
4 https://grobonet.com/.
5 https://webcmentarz.pl/.
6 http://mogily.pl/.
7 For example, https://www.pozegnaj.pl/, https://funer.com.pl/, https://uslugipo-grzebowe.com.pl/ and https://mementis.com.pl/.
8 https://portalkomunalny.pl/.

References

Act of 2 July 1947 on the *commemoration of the martyrdom of the Polish Nation and other Nations in Auschwitz* (JoL No. 52, item. 265, as amended).
Act of 24 February 2022 on the protection of national heritage related to the names of public space objects and monuments (Journal of Laws, item. 857).
Act of 28 March 1933 on war graves and cemeteries (Ct. JoL 2018, item. 2337).
Act of 7 May 1999 on the protection of the sites of former Nazi extermination camps (JoL 2015, item. 2120).
Bykowski Damian, Bober Dariusz 2015, "System geolokalizacji i upamiętnienia miejsc pochówku" (The web application for geolocalisation and commemoration a burial place), *Informatyka, Automatyka, Pomiary w Gospodarce i Ochronie Środowiska*, 5(3), 19–26.

Długozima Anna, Kosiacka-Beck Ewa 2020, "How to Enhance the Environmental Values of Contemporary Cemeteries in an Urban Context", *Sustainability*, 12(6), 1–19.

Jabłońska Lilianna, Sobczak Wioleta 2011, "Rynek chryzantem w Polsce w okresie Święta Wszystkich Świętych" (Polish market of chrysanthemum during the period of All Saints Day), *Roczniki Nauk Rolniczych*, 98(4), 66–76.

Kubica Grażyna 1986, "All Souls' Day in Polish Culture: Sacred or Secular?", *Journal of the Anthropological Society of Oxford*, XVII (2), 110–125.

Landowski Roman 2000, *Dawnych obyczajów rok cały. Między wiarą, tradycją i obrzędem* (Ancient customs a whole year. Between faith, tradition and ritual), Bernardinum, Pelplin.

Ogrodowska Barbara 2007, *Ocalić od zapomnienia Polskie tradycje i obyczaje rodzinne* (To save from oblivion. Polish family traditions and customs), Sport i Turystyka Muza SA, Warszawa.

Pietkiewicz Igor, 2012, "Burial rituals and cultural changes in the polish community – A qualitative study", *Polish Psychological Bulletin*, 43(4), 291–312.

Przybylska Lucyna, 2022, *Krzyże powypadkowe przy drogach w Polsce* (Memorial crosses along roads in Poland), Bernardinum, Pelplin.

Tanaś Sławoj 2020, "Sfera profanum Dnia Wszystkich Świętych wobec społecznego aspektu cmentarzy" (The profane sphere of All Saints' Day and the social aspect of cemeteries), *Turyzm*, 30/2, 103–112.

13 Protecting Funerary Heritage

Anna Długozima

With reference to the content of the previous chapters, civil cemeteries and graves – as opposed to war graves and cemeteries – are protected only by national legislation. However, war cemeteries are protected under international law. The domestic legal framework of cultural heritage protection in Poland is primarily set forth in the Act on the Protection and the Guardianship of Monuments (2003). The subjects of protection are, amongst others, cemeteries and places commemorating historical events, works of craftmanship, and archaeological monuments, in particular graveyards and barrows. The cemetery may be subject to historic protection as immovable property. Not only entire cemeteries but also individual fragments and single tombstones are subject to monument protection.

The overriding institutions involved in the protection of historic cemeteries are the Ministry of Culture and National Heritage, represented by the General Monument Inspector and Voivods, which in turn are represented by the Regional Monument Inspectors. The preservation and care of funerary heritage is financed mainly by a subsidy programme of the Ministry of Culture and National Heritage and Voivods' funds. Local government authorities are also responsible for the management of historical cemeteries by including the conservator's preservation area in the local spatial development plans and establishment of cultural parks (e.g., Cultural Park of The Jewish Cemetery in Żory established in 2004). Moreover, in the current legal order, municipalities are obliged to keep inventories of the monuments located on their territories, as well as to develop and implement municipal programmes of care for monuments.

The legal protection of graves, cemeteries and elements of necropolises takes place at the moment the site is added to the register of monuments. This register is the basic source of knowledge about the state of the heritage, and the entry is made on the basis of an administrative decision of the Regional Monument Inspector (Mazurek 2020).

DOI: 10.4324/9781003207634-13

The decision to add a site to the register has a number of legal effects. All works, such as the conservation of historical cemetery sculptures, gravestones and the location of new contemporary tombs, are subject to obtaining the permission of the abovementioned inspector. Being listed in this register also makes it possible to apply for subsidies for the protection, conservation works and preservation of the cemetery from the funds of the Ministry of Culture and National Heritage or voivods.

There are 4,196 cemeteries entered in the register of historic monuments in the territory of Poland. Of these, about 250 are Jewish, more than 60 are Evangelical-Augsburg, more than 500 are Roman Catholic, 50 are Orthodox, and more than 100 are municipal. Moreover, the register includes private family cemeteries, Muslim, Tartar, and Calvinist cemeteries (Mazurek 2020). It should be mentioned that apart from the register of monuments, there are also systems of municipality-level records of monuments. The main purpose of keeping records of cemeteries is to identify historic objects in the field and their factual and administrative documentation. There are 25,639 record cards of cemeteries in the NID collection. Cemetery cards were made mainly in the 1980s and 1990s, and almost ceased after the year 2000. The reason for this slowdown for cemeteries is insufficient funding to update the largely extant stock. Of the 123 sites with the status of a monument of history, granted by a decree of the President of the Republic of Poland at the request of the Ministry of Culture and National Heritage, three are established to protect unique sepulchral heritage: a group of historic religious cemeteries in Powązki, mizars in the villages of Bohoniki and Kruszyniany, and Radruż – an orthodox church complex that contains several hundred tombstones of folk sepulchral art from the so-called Brusno stonemasonry centre. Recognizing a structure as a monument of history does not entail any additional legal effects. The only effect is social awareness.

Between 1939 and 1950, the territory of present-day Poland was a place affected by large-scale population changes connected with the Shoah, mass expulsions, and refugees. There has been an almost complete replacement of the population of the border areas of postwar southeastern Poland (the Boykos and Lemkos) and Recovered Territories (inhabitants mainly of German nationality). Moreover, the Holocaust annihilated the Jewish diaspora living in Poland. The cemeteries of the former inhabitants were left abandoned, forgotten, and subject to destruction (Zawiła 2019).

Since the 1980s there has been a dynamic increase in the number of NGOs in Poland operating in the field of protecting and restoring sepulchral heritage: The Society for Preservation of Historical Monuments, The Association of Monument Conservators, The Magurycz Association, Guardians of Remembrance, The Cukerman

Gate Foundation, The Cultural Heritage Foundation, The Social Committee for Saving Old Cemeteries in Warmia and Mazury, The Association for the Protection of the Cultural Landscape (Sadyba), The Borussia Foundation. This increase can be related to an emerging civil society, which is an element of a maturing democracy (Zawiła 2019). By involving various stakeholders in the preservation of the funerary heritage, the NGOs hope that these restored cemeteries become part of the local social consciousness as places of rest, deserving of respect and quiet (see Figure 13.1).

The Magurycz Association is one of the longest-established NGOs in Poland, and its activities are focused on the rescue of sepulchral art. During its 36 years of activity, almost 3,000 tombstones in 150 cemeteries have been renovated. In 2020, the "(Un)Forgotten Cemeteries" Working Group has been set up under the Ombudsman to take action to preserve cultural heritage and care for cemeteries in Poland.

According to Jewish funeral heritage, a Citizens Committee for the Protection of Jewish Cemeteries and Cultural Monuments in Poland was founded in 1981. Twenty years later, the Foundation for the Preservation of Jewish Heritage in Poland was established. Caring for

Figure 13.1 Evangelical cemetery in former manor Zajączki (Warmińsko-Mazurskie Voivodeship) as an example of funerary heritage protected by inhabitants and foresters. Photograph by Anna Długozima.

Jewish cemeteries is one of the Foundation's undisputed priorities. Since in many cemeteries no matzevots have been preserved, the efforts to protect the Jewish sepulchral heritage very often consist of re-establishing the pre-war cemetery boundaries and putting up plaques commemorating the pre-war Jewish community. In 2018 The Ministry of Culture and National Heritage launched the programme "Marking Jewish Cemeteries on the Territory of the Republic of Poland". The main objective of the programme is to identify and restore the memory of forgotten Jewish cemeteries. Between 2018 and 2022, 33 sites were marked. A nationwide Coalition of Guardians of Jewish Cemeteries has also been formed to network and support local volunteers who care for Jewish cemeteries.

One of the forms of funerary heritage protection practised in Poland since the 1980s is the *lapidarium* – a place where old or artistically valuable tombstones are placed in situations where leaving them in their original place means their inevitable destruction. Examples of interesting lapidaries established in Poland to save the Lutherans' and Mennonites' legacy are sites in Kobylanka, Rodowo, Żychlin, Cyganek (Cemetery of 11 villages), Cisewo, Morzyczyn, Motaniec, Reptowo, Iwięcino, and Słowino.

In Poland, there is a growing interest in thanatotourism (Tanaś 2008), making tourist trails that include cemeteries an effective tool for protecting funerary heritage. The best examples are the route of the Eastern Front of WWI cemeteries in the Beskidy Mountains and the Chassidic Route. In northeastern Poland, on state-owned forest land, an effort has been made to valorise Protestant cemeteries for the purpose of developing a tourist trail (Sobotka, Długozima 2015).

References

Act on the protection and the guardianship of monuments, JoL 2003, No. 162, item. 1568.

Mazurek Anna 2020, "Administracyjnoprawna ochrona zabytkowych nekropolii jako miejsc dziedzictwa kulturowego" (Administrative and legal protection of historic necropolises as cultural heritage sites), *Ochrona Zabytków*, No. 1, 177–193.

Sobotka Sławomir, Długozima Anna 2015, "Evaluation and development opportunities of the disused Lutheran cemeteries within the Maskulińskie and Pisz forest divisions for thanatourism", *Tourism*, 25/1, 67–75.

Tanaś Sławoj 2008, *Przestrzeń turystyczna cmentarzy. Wstęp do tanatoturystyki* (Tourist space of cemeteries. Introduction to Thanatotourism), Wydawnictwo Uniwersytetu Łódzkiego, Łódź.

Zawiła Małgorzata 2019, *Dziedziczenie przedwojennych cmentarzy na terenach postmigracyjnych Polski* (Inheriting and perception of the pre-war cemeteries in the post-migration areas of Poland), Wydawnictwo Uniwersytetu Jagiellońskiego, Kraków.

Index